中外文稀有版本文献

《路易·波拿巴的雾月十八日》

②

英文版

【德】卡尔·马克思 ◎ 著

《路易·波拿巴的雾月十八日》的出版与传播

（代序）

恩格斯在1885年《路易·波拿巴的雾月十八日》（简称《雾月十八日》）第三版序言中指出："马克思立即写出一篇简练的讽刺作品，叙述了二月事变以来法国历史的全部进程的内在联系，揭示了12月2日的奇迹就是这种联系的自然和必然的结果，而他在这样做的时候对政变的主角除了给予其应得的蔑视以外，根本不需要采取别的态度。"[①] 尽管马克思直言《雾月十八日》是在形势的直接逼迫下写成的，但是"研究这部作品的写作过程，不仅可以窥探马克思的世界观的发展，而且可以瞥见他的创造性的实验"[②]。相比于维克多·雨果的《小拿破仑》、蒲鲁东的《从十二月二日政变看社会革命》，《雾月十八日》得到更为广泛的传播和影响。因而本文重点考察《雾月十八日》的写作过程及其出版遭遇、国内外传播及其深刻的影响。

一 《雾月十八日》的出版

在魏德迈到达纽约之后，1851年10月31日马克思致信建议他从事书籍出版事业，从《新莱茵报。民主派机关报》《新莱茵报。政治经济

---

① 《马克思恩格斯文集》第2卷，北京：人民出版社2009年版，第468页。
② 〔苏〕纳·维·库德里亚绍娃：《马克思创作〈路易·波拿巴的雾月十八日〉曾依据什么资料》，载《马克思恩格斯研究》1989年第2辑，第286页。

评论》选出最精彩的文章作为单行本出版。魏德迈在给马克思的信中痛骂小商人心理，说这种心理在哪里也不像在新大陆表现得这样令人作呕的露骨。此外，他准备从 1852 年 1 月初开始出版一个政治周刊。1851 年 12 月 16 日上午恩格斯收到魏德迈的信件，获悉魏德迈能够出版周刊并且要求自己在星期五晚上以前寄一篇文章给他。恩格斯认为："恰好在目前，那里正渴望看到对法国事件的评论和阐述，如果能够对局势作一个出色的阐述，那就能保证该刊从创刊号开始就获得成功。但困难也就在这里，而我又不得不像往常一样把重担压在你身上。……无论如何，在这方面你可以为他写一篇外交式的、有回旋余地的、划时代的文章。"① 1851 年 12 月 19 日，马克思致信魏德迈："现在我正坐下为你写一篇文章。你的约稿信来得太迟了，所以我今天不能完成。星期二（12 月 23 日）将从这里给你寄去：（1）卡·马克思的《路易·波拿巴的雾月十八日》……"② 魏德迈在回信中建议马克思为即将问世的政治周刊写一篇关于 1851 年政变的文章，就像马克思曾在他负责发行的《新莱茵报》上发表关于 1848 年革命的系列作品那样。

（一）马克思与恩格斯对法国局势的交流

在写作过程中，马克思不仅利用了英法两国的书刊和官方资料以及寄自巴黎的私人书信，特别是海涅的秘书莱因哈特从巴黎寄给马克思的若干信件。③ 莱因哈特阐述了巴黎各个阶层对于政变的不满和动荡情绪，论述了波拿巴政权的前景。"波拿巴在政变前和政变后毫无例外地搞坏了他和一切政党的关系以后，正从所推行的这种或那种笼络人心的措施（如扩大社会性工作，许诺对十二月二日的参加者实行大赦等）中寻求平衡。但是，只要他试图干点什么事以有利于某一个阶级，所

---

① 《马克思恩格斯全集》第 27 卷，北京：人民出版社 1972 年版，第 413 页。
② 《马克思恩格斯全集》第 27 卷，北京：人民出版社 1972 年版，第 617 页。
③ 对于资料来源的较为详细论述，参见《〈路易·波拿巴的雾月十八日〉的写作和出版情况》，《马克思恩格斯研究》1992 年第 8 期，第 201—204 页。

这一切就都成为不稳定的和无目的的了。"① 马克思在《雾月十八日》中直接引用了莱因哈特1852年2月15日信中基佐的名言"这是社会主义的完全而彻底的胜利!"和日拉丹夫人的话。莱因哈特在1851年7月到1852年10月这段时期写给马克思的信留下了7封,它们的主要内容是叙述和分析与1851年十二月二日政变有联系的法国政治事件。② 当然马克思认为莱因哈特是个怀疑论者,因为他不大看得起人民。莱因哈特在致马克思的信件中指出:"巴黎公众的情绪发生了显著的变化;如果说这种情绪还没有超出绝望的程度,那么这种绝望的确已经感觉出来了,而且具有更阴暗更普遍的性质。"③

很大程度上恩格斯对法国革命局势的判断塑造着马克思的革命思考,也反映出马克思恩格斯都以唯物史观审视法国革命的趋势与前景及其共同认识和理解。1846年9月,恩格斯曾经揭示过1830年后法国立法权的实质与历史命运。"在1830年革命后这个时期内,从来还没有出现过这样露骨的厚颜无耻和对社会舆论的蔑视。至少有3/5的议员是内阁的亲朋密友;换句话说,这些人不是大资本家、商人、巴黎交易所的铁路股票投机家、银行家和大工业家之流,就是他们的恭顺奴仆。现在的立法权比以前的任何立法权都更加体现出拉菲特在七月革命后第一天所说的话:'从今以后,统治法国的将是我们银行家了。'这是大金融贵族和haute bourgeoisie〔资产阶级巨头〕统治法国的最显著的证明。决定法国命运的不是土伊勒里宫,也不是贵族院,甚至也不是众议院,而是巴黎交易所。"④ 法国工人阶级为自己的生存而斗争,丢弃了对祖国的幻想。对于1848年六月革命,恩格斯乐观地指出:"'马赛曲'连同对于法国大革命的其他一切回忆一起消逝了。"⑤ 只有无产阶级是真

---

① 《马克思恩格斯全集》第28卷,北京:人民出版社1973年版,第498页。
② 〔苏〕纳·维·库德里亚绍娃:《马克思创作〈路易·波拿巴的雾月十八日〉曾依据什么资料》,载《马克思恩格斯研究》1989年第2辑,第292页。
③ 《马克思恩格斯全集》第28卷,北京:人民出版社1973年版,第496—497页。
④ 《马克思恩格斯全集》第4卷,北京:人民出版社1958年版,第30页。
⑤ 《马克思恩格斯全集》第5卷,北京:人民出版社1958年版,第137页。

正革命的阶级,然而流氓无产阶级则甘心于被人收买,干反动的勾当。恩格斯明确地指出流氓无产阶级的反动角色,成为工人受到残酷镇压的帮凶。"主要从巴黎流氓无产阶级中召募来的别动队,由于薪俸优厚,在短期内就成了每次都替当权者卖命的御用军。被组织起来的流氓无产阶级反对未组织起来的劳动无产阶级。果然不出所料,像那不勒斯的流浪汉供斐迪南驱使一样,巴黎的流氓无产阶级甘愿供资产阶级驱使。"①

资产者以前并不容忍乞丐、浪人、无赖、顽童和小偷为非作歹的行为,现在却宠爱这些流氓无产阶级,以便残酷地屠杀和镇压革命的巴黎工人。

恩格斯批评激进小资产阶级的软弱无力,无力采取革命的行动。"2月25日,当武装的无产阶级统治巴黎的时候,当可能得到一切的时候,不就是这些人只会说安慰人的漂亮话,而没有革命的行动,只会许诺和规劝,而不采取迅速和坚决的措施。"② 恩格斯认为,犹豫不决、幻想(自我牺牲)的陈词滥调、为了革命的模糊回忆而忘记革命的行动是整个激进小资产阶级的固有特征。"激进小资产者之所以带有社会主义情绪,只是因为他们清楚地看到自己即将灭亡,看到自己即将加入无产阶级的行列。他们不是作为小资产者、小量资本的所有者,而是作为未来的无产者在幻想劳动组织,幻想资本和劳动之间关系的变革。只要他们获得政权,他们很快就会忘掉劳动组织。因为政权,至少是在最初一些日子的陶醉中,会使他们看到有获得资本和从威胁他们的灭亡中得救的前景。只有当武装的无产者端着刺刀为他们作后盾的时候,他们才会想起自己昨天的同盟者。"③ 小资产阶级并不是革命的,而是保守的。"这里所谈的根本不是山岳党在宣言中极其郑重地宣布过的能拯救世界的某些琐屑措施。这里所谈的是社会革命,它将给法国人带来跟那些语无伦次的、已成为死板公式的词句完全不同的结果。这里所谈的是实现这一

---

① 《马克思恩格斯全集》第5卷,北京:人民出版社1958年版,第151页。
② 《马克思恩格斯全集》第6卷,北京:人民出版社1961年版,第663—664页。
③ 《马克思恩格斯全集》第6卷,北京:人民出版社1961年版,第665页。

革命所必需的毅力。问题在于小资产阶级既然已经一度表现了软弱无能以后，是否还能在它那里找到这种毅力。"① 小资产阶级只有不维护他们目前的利益，而是维护他们将来的来临时，才能站到无产阶级的立场上，才能体现出革命所需的毅力。

1850年11月，恩格斯回到曼彻斯特，当时正在阅读法国和英国历史学家所写的执政时代和帝国的历史，特别是从军事角度去阅读。马克思与恩格斯对法国政局的变化与趋势保持着密切的交流，讨论着法国政治变化的前景，嘲笑着路易·波拿巴。恩格斯在1851年2月12日致信马克思中指出："路易·拿破仑真是个蠢材！为了一百八十万法郎，他把自己对'选举法'的疑问出卖给了立法议会，而把自己出卖给了蒙塔郎贝尔，最后钱也没有拿到手。这样一个冒险家的确成不了什么事业。如果他在四个星期内让狡猾的阴谋家牵着自己的鼻子走，那么第五个星期他必定让人家用最愚蠢的方式把他完成的一切破坏无遗。要么做凯撒，要么做克里希！"② 1851年5月份，马克思和恩格斯愈来愈感觉波拿巴执政的机会最大。恩格斯在分析波拿巴政变的后果时指出："路易·拿破仑的统治并没有结束阶级之间的战争。它只是暂时中止了时时标志着这个或那个阶级夺取或保住政权的企图的流血冲突。"③

对于波拿巴政权的前景与原因，恩格斯认为，波拿巴的军事专制"在和平时期必然会引起新的军事政变并会促使在军队中出现国民议会的各个党派。没有任何出路，这个笑剧必然自行垮台。如果再出现商业危机，那就不堪设想了！"④ 无产阶级并不愿意为国民议会战斗，一直等到更加尖锐更加明确的冲突出现。"如果这一次无产阶级没有群起而战斗，那是因为他们完全意识到自己的懈怠和无力，并将以宿命论的驯顺态度屈从于共和国、帝国、复辟和新的革命这种一再的循环，直

---

① 《马克思恩格斯全集》第6卷，北京：人民出版社1961年版，第666页。
② 《马克思恩格斯全集》第27卷，北京：人民出版社1972年版，第208页。
③ 《马克思恩格斯全集》第11卷，北京：人民出版社1995年版，第266页。
④ 《马克思恩格斯全集》第27卷，北京：人民出版社1972年版，第408页。

到他们在比较安定的统治下经历了若干年的灾难而重新积聚起新的力量时为止。"①

恩格斯也强调暴力的重要性，也提及日拉丹的过分自信。"如果明年在法国爆发革命，神圣同盟至少要进到巴黎城下，这是毫无疑问的。我们的法国革命家虽然具有渊博的知识和罕见的精力，但甚至巴黎的堡垒和要塞围墙能否得到所需要的武器和粮食，也还是个大问题。而只要有两个堡垒，例如圣丹尼及其东邻最近的堡垒，被敌人夺去，那么巴黎和革命就会在新的事件爆发之前垮台。"② 恩格斯认为，日拉丹低估了波拿巴，但是国民议会的保守党很可能与体现行政权的波拿巴达成妥协，"虽然日拉丹也说，卡芬雅克现在是资产阶级群众的即秩序党的唯一真正的候选人，但是他自己却猛烈地攻击卡芬雅克和尚加尔涅，他的论战令人重新想起他同《国民报》作斗争的极盛时期。这个家伙正在法国进行广泛的鼓动，比整个山岳党人和红色分子一帮合起来所进行的鼓动还要广泛。波拿巴好像已不在话下了。不过，如果国民议会的保皇党多数派再度违反宪法，**以简单的**多数决定修改宪法，那么他们最终仍然会被迫——因为他们会丧失一切合法的支柱——同体现行政权的波拿巴达成妥协。在这种情况下，可能会弄到发生严重冲突的地步，因为卡芬雅克很难再度让人把到了他嘴边的东西夺去。"③

1851年12月3日，恩格斯在致信马克思时认为十二月十日政变是可笑的模仿剧："法国的历史已经进入了极其滑稽可笑的阶段。一个全世界最微不足道的人物，在和平时期，依靠心怀不满的士兵，根据到目前为止能作出的判断并没有遭到任何反抗，就演出了雾月十八日的可笑的模仿剧，还能有比这更有趣的事情吗！"④ 很显然，马克思的标题设置与对波拿巴的态度受到恩格斯的深刻影响，而且二人对此保持着相同

---

① 《马克思恩格斯全集》第27卷，北京：人民出版社1972年版，第410页。
② 《马克思恩格斯全集》第27卷，北京：人民出版社1972年版，第250页。
③ 《马克思恩格斯全集》第27卷，北京：人民出版社1972年版，第282页。
④ 《马克思恩格斯全集》第27卷，北京：人民出版社1972年版，第401页。

的看法。此外，恩格斯还比较了法国大革命时期拿破仑与波拿巴，强调波拿巴主义的专制色彩："现在甚至不再有什么国民议会可以破坏这个不被承认的英雄的伟大计划了；不会有了，至少在今天这头驴子像雾月十八日晚上的老拿破仑一样自由自在，一样无拘无束，一样绝对专制，他感到那样不受羁绊，以致不由得在各方面显出了驴子的本性。"① 恩格斯更进一步指出："就我们昨天所看到的而言，对人民是不能抱任何希望了，真好像是老黑格尔在坟墓里把历史当作世界精神来指导，并且真心诚意地使一切事件都出现两次，一次是作为伟大的悲剧出现，另一次是作为卑劣的笑剧出现。"② 马克思稍加改动和扩展，即将其运用到《雾月十八日》的首段，从总体上显示出马克思对波拿巴政变的认知和态度。恩格斯在12月10日和11日的两封信中揭示了巴黎工人没有大规模抵制这次政变的原因。③ "恩格斯在1852年1月、2月、3月写给马克思的许多信，或多或少的程度上都是对这次政变的分析评论。"④

　　大约1851年12月20日至1852年1月4日，恩格斯在伦敦期间与马克思当面讨论了法国政变问题。1852年2月至4月刊登在《寄语人民》上的恩格斯的《去年十二月法国无产者相对消极的真正原因》在内容上是与马克思的《雾月十八日》相衔接的。恩格斯也揭示了波拿巴政变成功的原因、本质及其固有的矛盾。⑤ 这组文章也表明马克思同恩格斯就《雾月十八日》中论述的问题诚挚地交换过看法。恩格斯的这组文章虽然扼要地集中论述工人阶级的策略，但实际上阐述的是《雾月十八日》的同一思想。⑥

---

① 《马克思恩格斯全集》第27卷，北京：人民出版社1972年版，第402页。
② 《马克思恩格斯全集》第27卷，北京：人民出版社1972年版，第403页。
③ 《马克思恩格斯全集》第27卷，北京：人民出版社1972年版，第408、410页。
④ 〔苏〕纳·维·库德里亚绍娃：《马克思创作〈路易·波拿巴的雾月十八日〉曾依据什么资料》，载《马克思恩格斯研究》1989年第2辑，第288页。
⑤ 《马克思恩格斯全集》第11卷，北京：人民出版社1995年版，第259—271页。
⑥ 《〈路易·波拿巴的雾月十八日〉的写作和出版情况》，载《马克思恩格斯研究》1992年第8期，第200页。

(二)《雾月十八日》的写作

波拿巴政变的悲喜剧困扰着马克思,以至于马克思并未立即回信恩格斯。马克思指出:"我被巴黎的这些悲喜剧事件弄得十分忙乱……我不能像维利希那样说:'真奇怪,巴黎方面竟什么也没有告诉我们!'我也不能像沙佩尔那样,老是拿着一杯啤酒在谢特奈尔酒馆里高谈阔论……所以他们决定等到事情'决定下来'以后再大踏步前进。"① 对于波拿巴政变的法国局势,马克思乐观地认为,"无论如何,我看改变是使局势好转了,而不是恶化了。波拿巴要比国民议会和它的将军们更容易对付。而国民议会的专政'已站在门外了'"。② 马克思明确地认为,波拿巴暂时取得了胜利,而且无产阶级保全了自己的力量。

当时马克思一家正处于生计艰难时期,而且马克思自己也饱受疾病的困扰,要做很大的努力才能工作。据燕妮回忆,马克思是在第恩街的一间小房里,在孩子们的吵闹声和家庭琐事搅扰下写完这本书的。她于3月转抄好手稿,并把它送出去。③ 马克思的女儿爱琳娜·马克思也曾经回忆:"事实上,就是他在索荷区第恩街写《雾月十八日》中的几章时,他也被三个孩子当做拉车的马,他们坐在他身后的椅子上,不停地用鞭子驱赶着他。"④

1852年1月1日,马克思致信魏德迈:"我现在才把文章寄给你,是因为工作不但受到当前急剧发展的事态的影响,而且在更大程度上还受到私事的干扰。从现在起开始正常了。"⑤ 然而正在1852年新年之际,由于恩格斯在伦敦挽留马克思狂饮了一顿,导致了燕妮对马克思的

---

① 《马克思恩格斯全集》第27卷,北京:人民出版社1972年版,第405页。
② 《马克思恩格斯全集》第27卷,北京:人民出版社1972年版,第406页。
③ 〔德〕燕妮·马克思:《动荡生活简记》,载中央编译局编译《回忆马克思》,北京:人民出版社2005年版,第61页。
④ 〔德〕爱琳娜·马克思:《卡尔·马克思》,载中央编译局编译《回忆马克思》,北京:人民出版社2005年版,第207页。
⑤ 《马克思恩格斯全集》第28卷,北京:人民出版社1973年版,第469页。

一些不满。由于重感冒，马克思病卧在床上，无法专心地撰写《雾月十八日》。1852年1月9日，燕妮告知魏德迈："我的丈夫一周来病得很重，几乎一直躺在床上。"① 正是在这种艰难的情况下，马克思完成了《雾月十八日》第二章内容的写作。1852年1月16日，马克思致信魏德迈指出："今天是我两个星期以来第一次下床。你可以看出，我的病是严重的，直到目前还没有痊愈。因此这星期我不能如愿把我论波拿巴的文章的第三篇寄给你。……我现在还非常虚弱，不能继续写了。"② 1852年1月19日，马克思开始下床了，20日又开始写东西了。

1852年1月23日，马克思再次向魏德迈表达了遗憾："遗憾得很，我的病还不允许我在这个星期给你，也就是给你的报纸写点东西。我**好不容易**才给德纳弄成一篇文章，他已有六个多星期没有收到我任何东西了。多少年来还没有一件事，甚至最近的法国丑事也没有像这该死的痔疮那样打破我的生活常规。但是现在我感到就会好起来，一个月内不得不离开图书馆，曾使我非常苦恼。"③ 1852年1月24日，马克思致恩格斯的信件中指出："你从这里走后，我给可怜的魏德迈自然只能寄去一篇文章。这次痔疮对我的折磨比法国革命还厉害。我要设法在下星期写出点东西。我的'臀部的'情况还不允许我去图书馆。" 1月30日、2月13日，马克思分别将稿件的第三章、第四章寄给魏德迈，然而马克思自己一旦投入写作便一发不可收拾，越写越多。正在这时，经济困境干扰着马克思，使他无法继续写作。1852年2月20日，马克思致信魏德迈："我这个星期不能寄任何东西给你，原因很简单，一个多星期以来，我陷入可恶的经济困境之中，以致我无法继续在图书馆从事研究，更不用说写文章了。"④ 3月5日，马克思寄出了第五章，3月25日终于把最后一部分原稿寄给了魏德迈。正是在3月25日致魏德迈的信件中，

---

① 《马克思恩格斯全集》第28卷，北京：人民出版社1973年版，第640页。
② 《马克思恩格斯全集》第28卷，北京：人民出版社1973年版，第473—474页。
③ 《马克思恩格斯全集》第28卷，北京：人民出版社1973年版，第475页。
④ 《马克思恩格斯全集》第28卷，北京：人民出版社1973年版，第492页。

马克思要求在第五篇的末尾加上如下的话:"然而波拿巴像阿革西拉乌斯回答国王亚奇斯那样回答了秩序党:'你把我看作蚂蚁,但是总有一天我会成为狮子的。'"① 然而魏德迈在 3 月 30 日的回信中告知,马克思的文稿没有出版的希望了。

(三)《雾月十八日》的出版

由于魏德迈缺乏资金,政治周刊的出版计划遭到了失败。② 事实上,马克思与恩格斯都担心任何妨碍出版的困难会发生。1852 年 1 月 1 日,马克思在致魏德迈的信中提醒道:"如果你由于资金困难不得不把自己的事业推迟一个较长的时间——**希望不会发生这种情况,**——那就请你把文章交给德纳,以便他把文章译成英文供他的报纸刊用。不过我希望这没有必要。"③ 魏德迈"写道:'从秋天以来,失业现象在这里空前严重,以致每一个新企业都遭到巨大的困难。而且,近来工人们受到各式各样的盘剥。最初是金克尔,接着是科苏特,而大多数人都愚蠢到宁可送一块钱给敌视他们的宣传,而不愿出一分钱来捍卫资金的利益。美国的土壤对人们起着一种极大的腐蚀作用,而同时人们却开始以为,他们比旧大陆的人们高瞻远瞩得多哩。'但是魏德迈并没有绝望,他希望能够使他的周刊以月刊的形式复活"④。

获悉《革命》无法出版的消息,马克思曾经建议魏德迈分印张或分篇出版。1852 年 2 月 13 日在马克思致信魏德迈的附言中,燕妮第一次提到马克思的建议:"我的丈夫认为,他的关于法国的一组文章(还有两篇要加进去),是最应时的东西,因此作为他在《评论》上发表的文章的续篇,也是最适于印小册子的材料。如果纽约某个出版商同德国

---

① 《马克思恩格斯全集》第 28 卷,北京:人民出版社 1973 年版,第 511 页。
② 对于《雾月十八日》在纽约出版的情况,参见《〈路易·波拿巴的雾月十八日〉的写作和出版情况》,载《马克思恩格斯研究》1992 年第 8 期,第 209—214 页。
③ 《马克思恩格斯全集》第 28 卷,北京:人民出版社 1973 年版,第 469—450 页。
④ 〔德〕梅林:《马克思传》,樊集译,北京:人民出版社 1985 年版,第 272—273 页。

有联系，那么可以指望在德国有相当大的销路。这部著作与其说是为美国倒不如说是为欧洲而写的。"① 2月20日，马克思在附言中再次强调："如果你的报纸不能出版，那么你是否能把我的小册子分印张出版或者像我给你寄去的那样分篇出版？否则时间会拖得太长。"② 1852年2月27日，燕妮致信魏德迈时指出，马克思"请您马上把他的论拿破仑的文章的五篇寄回，如果您不能刊登的话。也许，我们能把它们译成法文出版，虽然放弃德文的确很可惜"。"我的丈夫认为，最好您能在美国出版这东西，因为它肯定能收回成本；并且最好还能在德国推销，因为它对当前最重大的事件作出了历史的评价。""为了不致拖延过久，您可以将每一篇单独刊登，因为这些东西非常引人注意。然后可以把所有这些并在一起。今天寄上第五篇，下星期五他将寄上第六篇——结尾部分。我再说一遍，**请您尽力将这部著作印成小册子**。如果办不到，请您把它寄回，——无论如何必须把它出版。"③

魏德迈在1852年4月9日的信件中提及："出版这本小册子所面临的困难，终于因得到意料之外的帮助而克服了。在我上一次的信发出以后，我遇到了我们法兰克福的一个工人，他是一个裁缝，今年夏天刚刚来到这儿。他把自己省下来的四十美元全部交给了我，供我使用。"④ 马克思在致阿道夫·克路斯的信件中谈及《雾月十八日》即将出版的欣喜之情，也非常满意："你那封令人感到《波拿巴》有出版希望的信（4月19日接到的），使我特别高兴，因为对于我的妻子的非常柔软的性格来说，这件事一定又会使她振奋起来……"⑤ 1852年5月，魏德迈以单行本形式将这部论著作为不定期刊物《革命》的第一期出版，却

---

① 《马克思恩格斯全集》第28卷，北京：人民出版社1973年版，第490页。
② 《马克思恩格斯全集》第28卷，北京：人民出版社1973年版，第495页。
③ 《马克思恩格斯全集》第28卷，北京：人民出版社1973年版，第643—644页。
④ 约瑟夫·魏德迈致马克思的信（1852年4月9日），参见梅林：《新近为卡·马克思和弗·恩格斯的传记而写的文章》，载《新时代》德文版第25卷，第二册，第103页；转引自因里希·格姆科夫等：《马克思传》，侯廷镇等译，北京：人民出版社2000年版，第176页。
⑤ 《马克思恩格斯全集》第28卷，北京：人民出版社1973年版，第518页。

在扉页和自己写的前言中误将标题写成了《路易·拿破仑的雾月十八日》。① 恩格斯在评价《雾月十八日》的出版技术工作时指出："很可惜铅字太小，开本太大，这给阅读增添很大困难，特别是在碰到歪曲意思的刊误的时候，当然，由于经费不足，要避免这种情况是不可能的。"②

二 《雾月十八日》的世界传播

1851年12月2日波拿巴政变是当时欧洲政治的重要事件，成为很多著作的主题。其中维克多·雨果的《小拿破仑》、蒲鲁东的《从十二月二日政变看社会革命》两部著作当时特别有名，而且给作者带来了丰厚的报酬，但是《雾月十八日》却并未如此幸运。然而时过境迁，它们的命运却发生了相反的变化。正如梅林所说的："马克思的著作问世时，和那两个更幸运的姊妹相比就好像灰姑娘一样。但是那两部著作早已被遗忘的尘埃掩盖了，而马克思的著作却至今仍然放射着不朽的光辉。在这部闪烁着智慧和机智的著作中，马克思以前无古人的技巧，以历史唯物主义的观点透彻地分析了当代的事件。这部著作的形式和它的内容一样辉煌。"③

（一）"不合时宜"的遭遇与转折

相比于《法兰西阶级斗争》和《科隆共产党人案件》，《雾月十八日》现在得到更为广泛的传播。然而在马克思时代事情却截然相反。1852年5月25日前后，《雾月十八日》开始在美国销售。事与愿违，销路极差。然而伦敦同盟支部的成员以及马克思和恩格斯在英国和欧洲

---

① 吴学琴主编：《马克思主义著作选读》，合肥：安徽人民出版社2008年版，第270页。
② 《马克思恩格斯全集》第28卷，北京：人民出版社1973年版，第531页。
③ 〔德〕梅林：《马克思传》，樊集译，北京：人民出版社1985年版，第271页。

大陆上的为数众多的朋友和熟人都收到了《雾月十八日》。① 当时魏德迈印刷了1000份《雾月十八日》，将其中近三分之一都寄往欧洲；数百份输送到德国，但并没有在真正的书籍市场上出售过。1852年1月23日，恩格斯致信魏德迈中曾提到《革命》的发行问题，"五十本《革命》太多了，可能要付很大一笔钱，即每次要付四先令甚至更多的钱。由于到处进行逮捕，人们各奔东西等，以及由于德国的出版法，在这里只能指望有少数的订户，而在德国——也许只有在汉堡才能指望有几个订户。因此分发试刊没有什么用处。"②

大概从1852年8月初，马克思设法安排《雾月十八日》在德国出版，也试图出版英文版。在1852年8月至9月间，马克思试图在德国出版此书，但一切尝试都未成功。马克思曾经在1869年《雾月十八日》第二版序言中提到："当我向一个行为极端激进的德国书商建议销售这种刊物时，他带着真正的道义上的恐惧拒绝了这种'不合时宜的要求'。"③ 保尔·拉法格指出："他的《雾月十八日》完全无人注意，这部著作证明1848年所有的历史学家和政论家，只有马克思一个人才了解1851年12月2日那次政变的原因和结果。虽然这本书是谈论当前的重大问题，但却没有一家资产阶级的报纸提到过它。"④ 1852年9月，马克思希望用英文出版《雾月十八日》，以扩大《雾月十八日》在世界范围的影响。当时马克思找到共产主义同盟盟员皮佩尔翻译第一章，并请求琼斯翻译这部著作，并希望在其主办的《人民报》上刊登。琼斯起初答应了，但是并没有兑现诺言，因而没有出版。恩格斯邀请共产主义者同盟盟员皮佩尔翻译，并经恩格斯润饰过的《雾月十八日》在10月底正式出版英译本，但同样销路不畅。当马克思收到由魏德迈在纽约

---

① 《〈路易·波拿巴的雾月十八日〉的写作和出版情况》，载《马克思恩格斯研究》1992年第8期，第214、217页。
② 《马克思恩格斯全集》第28卷，北京：人民出版社1973年版，第479页。
③ 《马克思恩格斯文集》第2卷，北京：人民出版社2009年版，第465页。
④ 〔德〕保尔·拉法格：《回忆马克思》，载中央编译局编译《回忆马克思》，北京：人民出版社2005年版，第202页。

出版的《雾月十八日》后，1852年12月11日和18日琼斯两次在《人民报》上发表了对此书的评论，这是《雾月十八日》最早的评论性文章。

直到1869年书籍市场的需求以及德国朋友的催促，才促使马克思安排汉堡出版商奥·迈斯纳在汉堡出版了第二版。当时俾斯麦在发动普法战争之前，企图效仿波拿巴的政变。马克思这时决定再版《雾月十八日》。1869年1月底，马克思在给恩格斯的信件中，谈及他准备重版《雾月十八日》，并告诉恩格斯，迈斯纳愿意承担该书的出版工作。1869年5月21日马克思致信恩格斯："迈斯纳一星期前给我寄来《雾月十八日》的第一个印张，并保证说，现在工作将'迅速'进行。"① 再版前，马克思重新审订了原文，改正了印刷错误，删去了重复的语句，节略了某些段落，将书名改为《路易·波拿巴的雾月十八日》。马克思于6月中旬才收到最后一批校样，6月23日撰写了序言并寄给迈斯纳。迈斯纳收到马克思寄来的校样和序言后，于7月20日在汉堡出版了《雾月十八日》德文版。

德国资产阶级报刊对《雾月十八日》新版竭力保持沉默。德国《人民报》只是在1870年8月16日才发表了该书出版的消息，同时刊登了序言。《雾月十八日》新版出版后，马克思立即寄给恩格斯数本，7月24日当恩格斯收到书后在给马克思的回信中称赞"这本书装帧很好，没有印错的字，读起来好得多。序言很好"②。

在《雾月十八日》中，马克思无情地控诉了路易·波拿巴这个暴发户，因此这本书要在法国出版，是根本不可想象的。由于在波拿巴政变之后紧接着发生了科隆共产党人案件，马克思要找到一个出版人就更加困难了。③ 1885年7月《雾月十八日》第三版出版后，恩格斯于同年

---

① 《马克思恩格斯全集》第32卷，北京：人民出版社1974年版，第302页。
② 李佩龙等：《〈路易·波拿巴的雾月十八日〉的写作、出版和传播》，载《宁夏大学学报（人文社会科学版）》1983年第1期，第18页。
③ 〔德〕梅林：《马克思传》，樊集译，北京：人民出版社1985年版，第275页。

7月至8月间开始审阅由法国社会主义者爱·福尔坦翻译的《雾月十八日》法文版。恩格斯与福尔坦通信，商谈关于在法国工人党机关报《社会主义者报》上发表这一译文的可能性。福尔坦知道《雾月十八日》是描写法国1848—1852年杰出的历史著作，所以想把它译成法文。此外，拉维涅也在翻译，但是恩格斯还是决定采用福尔坦的译本。法文本终于在1891年1月发表在法国《社会主义者报》上，在利尔德劳利出版社出版了单行本。①

即使如此，"不合时宜"的著作也在马克思主义者中影响广泛，受到了极大的关注。克路斯和魏德迈在其文章中多次援引《雾月十八日》并注明引自马克思的这部著作。1860年，卡尔·福格特还在美国一些德文地方小报上与之进行论战。19世纪60年代，马克思的《雾月十八日》不仅对于捍卫共产主义政党独立的政治立场，而且为反对波拿巴主义提供原则的和科学的论据，具有重大的现实意义。1862年以来，俾斯麦在普鲁士推行一项实质上是波拿巴主义的政策。② 作为马克思的亲密合作者恩格斯充分强调《雾月十八日》的意义，在《雾月十八日》第三版序言中明确地指出："的确，这是一部天才的著作。"③《雾月十八日》被视为验证马克思的唯物史观的范例，也被赋予科学的内涵。在《法兰西阶级斗争》和《雾月十八日》中，马克思是"用他的唯物主义观点一定从经济状况出发来说明一段现代历史的初次尝试"④。

1896年，德国和国际工人运动的著名活动家威廉·李卜克内西指出："马克思在《路易·波拿巴的雾月十八日》中为1851年12月2日的政变立了一块耻辱的碑石，就像但丁的《恐怖的三重唱》那样永恒

---

① 李佩龙等：《〈路易·波拿巴的雾月十八日〉的写作、出版和传播》，载《宁夏大学学报（人文社会科学版）》1983年第1期，第18页。
② 《〈路易·波拿巴的雾月十八日〉的写作和出版情况》，载《马克思恩格斯研究》1992年第8期，第215—216、221页。
③ 《马克思恩格斯文集》第2卷，北京：人民出版社2009年版，第468页。
④ 《马克思恩格斯全集》第22卷，北京：人民出版社1965年版，第591页。

不朽。"① "能够说《路易·波拿巴的雾月十八日》不能理解吗？难道直飞目标而深深刺入肉体的箭不能理解吗？难道妙手掷出、正中敌人心窝的投枪不能理解吗？《路易·波拿巴的雾月十八日》的语言就是箭和投枪，它的风格是用火烙，用刀杀。如果憎恨、轻蔑、对自由的热爱曾经在什么地方用燃烧、破坏和激昂的语言表达过，那就是在《路易·波拿巴的雾月十八日》这部著作中。这部著作把塔西佗的严肃的愤怒、尤维纳利斯的尖刻的讽刺和但丁的神圣的怒火综合在一起了。这种风格在这里就是stilus，即最初罗马人拿在手里的那种用以书写和刺戳的尖锐钢刀。这种风格是一把真正刺中心窝的匕首。"② 第一部《马克思传》的作者梅林视《雾月十八日》为马克思的小部头历史著作宝库中最晶莹灿烂的宝石。梅林认为："在这部闪烁着智慧和机智的著作中，马克思以前无古人的技巧，从历史唯物主义的观点透彻地分析了当代的事件，这部著作的形式和它的内容一样辉煌。"③

意大利第一个马克思主义哲学家拉布里奥拉因撰写《纪念〈共产党宣言〉》，而被恩格斯称之为"严肃的马克思主义者"。1896 年 3 月，拉布里奥拉指出了《雾月十八日》对于理解唯物史观的意义："正是他作为这个学说的基本原理的第一个和主要的创造者，很快地把这个学说变成政治理解的工具，成为 1848—1849 年革命时期的首屈一指的政论家。稍后，他在他的著作《路易·波拿巴的雾月十八日》中最彻底地运用了这个学说；就是在许多年和多次再版后的今天，我们可以说，这部著作——除了一些小的细节和个别的错误预言——不需要作任何修正和补充。"④ 拉布里奥拉认为："阐述路易·波拿巴的雾月十八日的著作

---

① 〔德〕威廉·李卜克内西：《纪念卡尔·马克思——生平与回忆》，载中央编译局编译《回忆马克思》，北京：人民出版社 2005 年版，第 56 页。
② 〔德〕威廉·李卜克内西：《纪念卡尔·马克思——生平与回忆》，载中央编译局编译《回忆马克思》，北京：人民出版社 2005 年版，第 31 页。
③ 〔德〕梅林：《马克思传》，樊集等译，北京：人民出版社 1965 年版，第 278 页。
④ 〔意〕安东尼奥·拉布里奥拉：《关于历史唯物主义》，杨启遵等译，北京：人民出版社 1981 年，第 133 页。

则是把新的历史观运用于有严格时间界限的一系列事实的第一个尝试。"① 马克思在《雾月十八日》中所提及的集团、霸权以及领导权等概念深刻地影响着意大利共产党创始人之一葛兰西。葛兰西提及《雾月十八日》时认为:"有人说,政治和意识形态的任何一次波动都可以当作基础的直接反映来加以描述和说明,并把这说成是历史唯物主义的一条基本原理。对于这种主张,必须当作一种原始的幼稚病从理论上加以驳斥,同时还要用具体的政治和历史著作葛兰西的作者马克思提供的真凭实据在实践中大力反对。从这一角度来看,特别重要的著作有《雾月十八日》和关于东方问题的文章,以及其他的论著(《德国的革命和反革命》《法兰西内战》)和一些短文。"②

在苏东共产党人中,列宁认为,与《共产党宣言》相比,马克思在《雾月十八日》中的精彩论述向前迈进了一大步。"在那里,国家问题还提得非常抽象,只用了最一般的概念和说法。在这里,问题提得具体了,并且作出了非常准确、明确、实际而具体的结论:过去一切革命都是使国家机器更加完备,而这个机器是必须打碎,必须摧毁的。这个结论是马克思主义国家学说中主要的基本的东西。"马克思的学说在这里也像其他任何时候一样,是由深刻的哲学世界观和丰富的历史知识阐明的经验总结。③ 克莱恩重点解读了"革命是历史的火车头"的论断以及无产阶级专政学说。他认为马克思以说明现代史的形式对革命事件进行广泛的研究,这种研究"也就失去了革命日报通过每日干预运动和直接成为运动的喉舌所具有的优点"。④《雾月十八日》对各种国家形式的转换及其原因以及对于国家机器的作用的研究,使马克思得出了无产阶级专政的本质的新结论。

---

① 〔意〕安东尼奥·拉布里奥拉:《关于历史唯物主义》,杨启遴等译,北京:人民出版社1981年,第27页。
② 〔意〕葛兰西:《葛兰西文选》,李鹏程编,北京:人民出版社2008年版,第236页。
③ 《列宁选集》第3卷,北京:人民出版社1995年版,第133—134页。
④ 〔东德〕马·克莱恩:《马克思主义哲学史》,北京:中国人民大学出版社1983年版,第338页。

在《雾月十八日》一书中，马克思以法兰西共和国为例，证明在资产阶级共和国的范围内，不可能消除工人阶级受剥削的现象在这部著作中，他第一次表达出这样一种思想，即无产阶级在革命胜利以后，不应该接过反动的、资产阶级的国家机器及其一切军事的、官僚主义的、为压迫人民群众而建立的机构，而是必须把国家机器砸碎。在无产阶级领导下，摧毁旧的国家机器，建立新的国家权力机关，实现从资本主义社会到共产主义社会的过渡——马克思把这些总称为"无产阶级专政"。①

（二）《雾月十八日》的广泛传播

《雾月十八日》出版后，当时一些评价本书的作者一般也把这部著作仅仅看成是分析法国事件及形势的政治论著。魏德迈所写的介绍文章指出："卡尔·马克思在《纽约论坛报》上发表题为〈德国革命与反革命〉的连载文章（这些论文是恩格斯写的，发表时用的是马克思名字——引者注），在文章中他描述了德国革命发展的当前形势。他用类似的方式在他的〈雾月十八日〉中叙述了法国的形势。"② 另一个作者埃卡留斯则指出，这本书"为波拿巴篡权的历史提出了不仅是第一个，而且是唯一的一个有权威的说明"。它"是唯一的一部同时既满足历史的要求，又满足当代人对理解所从事的革命运动的需要的著作"③。但是他们还没有指出这部著作的重大意义，更没有以方法论为指导对其进行诠释。

《雾月十八日》传播过程的一个重要事件是《雾月十八日》英译本的出版。1897年9月12日至11月14日，丹尼尔·德利昂（Daniel De

---

① 〔德〕海因里希·格姆科夫等：《马克思传》，侯廷镇等译，北京：人民出版社2000年版，第175—176页。
② 〔德〕约瑟夫·魏德迈：《路易·波拿巴的雾月十八日》一书序言，载《约瑟夫·魏德迈——美国社会主义的先驱》一书的附录。
③ 〔德〕格奥尔格·埃卡留斯：《政变文献评价》，载《马列著作编译资料》第8辑，北京：人民出版社1980年版，第19、5页。

Leon）将《雾月十八日》翻译成英文，以连载的方式发表在美国社会主义劳动党官方机构《人民报》（The People）周刊上。美国共产党主办的纽约国际出版公司（1935年、1963年、1972年、1987年等重印）在1897年12月首次出版了英文版本，① 而且指出西奥多·罗斯福与路易·波拿巴的惊人相似之处。德利昂在译者序言中指出，《雾月十八日》是马克思最深邃且富有才气的专题论文之一，是最优秀的历史著作之一。专门出版马克思主义著作的芝加哥查尔斯·克尔公司（1913年再版）、密歇根大学图书馆（1926年再版）分别在1907年出版了《雾月十八日》；艾伦＆安文公司在1926年（1939年、1943年再版）出版了《雾月十八日》。②

《雾月十八日》最早的俄文版是1894年在日内瓦出版的，同时恩格斯的序言也刊登在该书的第一版上。1905年至1906年由克里切夫斯基翻译的《雾月十八日》俄文版在日内瓦出版。1932年，苏联出版了《雾月十八日》，而且这个版本是把马克思自己在这部著作第二版去掉了的部分完全保存下来的唯一版本。1940年，苏联马克思恩格斯学院又出版了根据两卷集翻印的新版《雾月十八日》。③ 纽约劳动新闻公司1951年、阿普尔顿世纪调查公司1955年分别出版了《雾月十八日》。国际图书有限公司、中央图书有限公司分别在1969年、1977年出版了《雾月十八日》。

三 《雾月十八日》在中国的传播与影响

《雾月十八日》在中国有着较长的出版和传播史并产生了一定的影

---

① Karl Marx, *The Eighteenth Brumaire of Louis Bonaparte*, New York: the International Publishing Comoany, 1897.
② Karl Marx, *The Eighteenth Brumaire of Louis Bonaparte*, Chicago: Charles H.Kerr Company, 1907; *The Eighteenth Brumaire of Louis Bonaparte*, University of Michigan Library, 1907; *The Eighteenth Brumaire of Louis Bonaparte*, London: G.Allen & Unwin,Ltd., 1926.
③ 李佩龙等：《〈路易·波拿巴的雾月十八日〉的写作、出版和传播》，载《宁夏大学学报》（人文社会科学版）1983年第1期，第18页。

响。1919年12月,胡汉民在国民党理论刊物《建设》杂志发表《唯物史观批评之批评》一文节译了《雾月十八日》(当时译为《法兰西政变论文》),是最早见诸中文的节译本,为《雾月十八日》所蕴含的唯物史观、社会心理观在中国的传播提供了当时最为详尽的原文。① 1920年3月,李大钊倡导成立了"北京大学马克斯学说研究会"。那时研究会已有马克思主义的英文书籍四十余种,中文书籍二十余种,其中英文书籍包括《雾月十八日》。②《雾月十八日》最早的中译本是由陈仲涛翻译的《拿破仑第三政变记》,由上海江南书店在1930年5月出版的。③ 吴黎平(吴亮平的笔名)在其编译的《辩证法唯物论与唯物史观》中附录三《唯物史观研究大纲》中将陈仲涛所翻译的版本列为理解马克思主义社会发展、社会变革、个人在历史中的作用、唯物史观意义等方面的补充参考书。这对于《雾月十八日》在中国的传播起到了不可低估的作用。

1938年5月5日是马克思诞辰120周年纪念日,中共中央在延安建立了第一所马列学院(历史上第一个专门编译马列著作的机构),不久又建立了中共中央出版发行部,统一领导中共的出版发行工作。中央出版发行部以"解放社"的名义出版《马克思恩格斯丛书》,其中包括《拿破仑第三政变记》。1940年柯柏年译、吴黎平校的《拿破仑第三政变记》单行本在解放出版社出版。④ 赵俪生也讲述了其与《雾月十八日》的机缘。"在一九四零年春,我在西安偶尔从旧书摊上买到一本著着一位日本人姓名的伦敦版英译的《拿破仑第三政变记》。买后不久,立刻就动手翻译。译到一多半时,柯译本出版的消息便在重庆的《大公

---

① 李其驹:《马克思主义哲学在中国》,上海:上海人民出版社1991年版,第77—78页。

② 胡永钦等:《马克思恩格斯著作在中国传播的历史概述》,载《马克思恩格斯著作在中国的传播》,北京:人民出版社1983年版,第252页。

③ 参见上海出版大事记,http://www.shtong.gov.cn/node2/node2245/node4521/node29047/userobject1ai54450.html。

④ 〔德〕马克思:《拿破仑第三政变记》,柯柏年译,吴黎平校,延安:延安解放出版社1940年版。

报》和《新华日报》上刊出了。因此，我中止了翻译。那多半部的译稿在某次特务搜查中埋在砖底下的土里，后来竟完全朽烂了。这便是我与《拿破仑第三政变记》一书的因缘。"①

柯柏年按英文本并对照德文本译出《拿破仑第三政变记》，此后吴黎平按俄文本、英文本并参照德文本校对。② 尽管当时柯柏年在译本中列出了《雾月十八日》的英文标题，但是由于大家将其意译为《拿破仑第三政变记》而采取从众的态度，却将英文标题翻译为《路易•波拿巴底二月十八日》。该版本收录了马克思为第二版撰写的序言以及恩格斯为第三版撰写的序言。1940年8月，上海生活书店以"世界学术名著译丛"名义出版翻印或新译解放社出版的马克思恩格斯著作，其书名仍为《拿破仑第三政变记》。"当年每本书出版时印数可能有两千册左右。纸张多用马兰草纸，质量不好，只有发给中央委员们的书才用白报纸印，我们译者也可拿到一本白报纸本的赠书。我们的书在解放社出版后，往往很快就在重庆重印出版。"③ 柯柏年等在《译校者关于本书内容的一点说明》中高度评价了其意义。

> 在《拿破仑第三政变记》这书中，马克思如此英明地深刻地分析了法国这一时期的历史事变，如此具体地光辉地运用唯物史观的伟大理论，使得这一著作（和马克思的其他著作一样）虽然到现在差不多经过了九十年，还不仅没有丝毫失而反是日益显示其内容的正确与意义的伟大。这真是一部万古不磨的、百读不厌的名著。书上的文字是非常美丽的、有力的。在文字上说，这

---

① 赵俪生：《略评〈拿破仑第三政变记〉柯译本》，载《文史学的新探索》，上海：海燕书店1951年版，第187页。
② 杨荟娟：《抗日战争时期马列著作翻译的特点》，载《高校讲坛》2010年第19期。
③ 何锡麟：《回忆在延安翻译马列经典著作的情况》，载《马克思恩格斯著作在中国的传播》，北京：人民出版社1983年版，第129页。

部名著也可在文学上占最高的位置。①

对于《法兰西阶级斗争》和《拿破仑第三政变记》两本书,柯柏年曾回忆道:"有种论点认为,这两本书不是马克思的主要著作。其实,恰恰相反。马克思正是在这两本书里应用他的唯物史观剖析了他所处时代的重大事件。如果我们要学习马克思的理论,学习他如何应用其理论,那就必须仔细钻研这两本书。特别值得注意的是,恩格斯为《拿破仑第三政变记》所写的绪论。在这篇绪论里,恩格斯用唯物史观解释了法、德两国从十九世纪中期到十九世纪末期这几十年的历史,并对未来的革命做了分析和预见。"②

抗战胜利后,1947年9月,这本书由解放社出版了"胜利后的一版"。新中国成立后,重印的《雾月十八日》仍是上述"胜利后的一版"。1949年,哈尔滨的新华书店、北京的人民出版社、上海的光华书店等再次以《拿破仑第三政变记》为书名出版了《雾月十八日》。特别是,人民出版社在1953年、1954年两次印刷了该书。同年马列学院编写了《关于学习"拿破仑第三政变记"的参考材料》,编者在其后记中强调"这本书不甚易读,尤其是书中用典甚多,而且都是我们所不甚熟悉的外国典故,若对于这些典故不能了解,也就很难领会马克思的文章的妙处,因而障碍着领会文件的精神实质"。这些书在新中国成立后都曾再版或重印,但后来在有了中央编译局的译本后就不再印行了。

1950年12月人民出版社成立以后,马列著作的编辑出版工作开始有了集中统一的规划。一方面把过去的译本(包括解放社版和三联书店版)重新校订后统一用人民出版社的名义出版;一方面组织翻译新的译本,苏联外国文书籍出版社的版本也经过原译者校订译文后重新排印出

---

① 〔德〕马克思:《拿破仑第三政变记》,柯柏年译,吴黎平校,延安:延安解放出版社1940年版,第4页。

② 柯柏年:《我译马克思和恩格斯著作的简单经历》,载《马克思恩格斯著作在中国的传播》,北京:人民出版社1983年版,第32页。

版。1951年至1953年间,除人民出版社外,其他数家出版社也零星出版过一些马列著作。1953年以后马列著作基本上都统一由人民出版社出版了。《马克思恩格斯文选》第1卷集中编载了马克思的关于19世纪法国历史的三篇著作,以"路易·波拿巴政变记"为题名收录了《雾月十八日》的全文,视其为运用历史唯物主义方法分析具体历史事变的光辉范例。① 1955年2月26日,《人民日报》第三版对《马克思恩格斯文选》第1卷内容进行了介绍,包括《雾月十八日》。

1953年1月,中共中央成立了马克思恩格斯列宁斯大林著作编译局(简称中央编译局),其任务是有系统有计划地翻译马恩列斯的全部著作。中央编译局根据1955年开始出版的《马克思恩格斯全集》俄文第二版并参照德文原著译出的《马克思恩格斯全集》(第8卷)中文第一版收入了《雾月十八日》一文。《马克思恩格斯全集》俄文第二版所收的《雾月十八日》是根据1869年德文版本翻译的。编者援引了苏共中央马克思列宁主义研究院的《第八卷说明》指出,《雾月十八日》"是科学共产主义的最卓越的著作之一。这一分析历史事件并从理论上加以概括的天才著作,同时也是革命政论的真正杰作"②。特别是,编译者在《马克思恩格斯全集》(第8卷)中文第一版中首次根据原著标题译为"路易·波拿巴的雾月十八日",但并没有将马克思、恩格斯分别所写的两个序言编译在内。1962年,人民出版社据此出版了《路易·波拿巴的雾月十八日》一书,把1954年出版的《马克思恩格斯文选》中马克思、恩格斯的两篇序言其纳入此书中。③

1958年,中国青年出版社编辑出版的《马克思恩格斯列宁斯大林著作介绍》中介绍了《雾月十八日》历史背景、主要内容以及学习意义。编者认为:"这是《法兰西阶级斗争》一书的续篇,不仅科学总结了一八四八年法国革命历史经验,而且在科学社会主义理论方面作出了

---

① 《马克思恩格斯文选》第1卷,北京:人民出版社1954年版,第219—321页。
② 《马克思恩格斯全集》第8卷,北京:人民出版社1961年版,第XIII页。
③ 《路易·波拿巴的雾月十八日》,北京:人民出版社1962年版。

关于打碎旧国家机器的新结论，论述了工农联盟等重要原理。"① 编者强调《雾月十八日》在马克思主义发展史上的重要地位，对于全世界无产阶级革命实践的指导意义，视其为分析历史事件并从理论上加以概括的天才著作，是科学社会主义的一篇重要著作。

《马克思恩格斯选集》第1—4卷是中央编译局根据《马克思恩格斯全集》中文版选编，收录了马克思和恩格斯在各个时期的重要著作110篇，书信96封，共180万字。《马克思恩格斯选集》最早是重印苏联出版的谢唯真校订的《马克思恩格斯文选》两卷集，中央编译局编译的第一版四卷本《马克思恩格斯选集》是1966年6月出版的。当时文化大革命刚刚爆发，没有好好发行。1971年，在全国出版工作座谈会上，周恩来总理指示要出版马克思恩格斯和列宁的两部选集。中央编译局遵照周总理的指示，于1972年将编校后的《马克思恩格斯选集》第1—4卷交人民出版社出版，因1966年的版本基本没有发行，故这部《马克思恩格斯选集》就作为第一版第二次印刷。编者认为："在这部著作里，马克思运用唯物史观，特别是阶级和阶级斗争的理论，深刻地分析了一八四八年法国革命的几个阶段，科学地阐明了路易·波拿巴政变的原因、实质及其结局，进一步发展了马克思主义国家学说和工农联盟的原理，第一次提出了关于胜利的无产阶级必须打碎资产阶级国家机器的结论。"②

改革开放新时期，中央编译局根据党中央要求适应新时期马克思主义中国化的需要，为深入学习和研究马克思主义理论提供译文更准确、资料更翔实的马恩原著，决定编译一部中国版的《马克思恩格斯全集》，即《全集》第二版（即MECA版，又称国际版）。这个历史考证版收集的马克思恩格斯著作完全是他们的原始文字，主要是德文，也有

---

① 《马克思恩格斯列宁斯大林著作介绍》，北京：中国青年出版社1958年版，第85页。
② 《〈马克思恩格斯选集〉简要介绍》，沈阳：辽宁人民出版社1974年版，第94页。

英文、法文、意大利文、西班牙文等①。中央编译局完全按照马克思恩格斯的原文翻译。《马克思恩格斯全集》（第11卷）收入马克思和恩格斯在1851年8月至1853年3月所写的政治论著、时事评论、声明和文件，包括《雾月十八日》。② 在该版中，编者添加了《雾月十八日》1852年版本中部分内容的注释。1995年，在纪念恩格斯逝世一百周年之际，中央编译局又重编出版了《马克思恩格斯选集》四卷本的第二版，也就是拨改革开放以后的新版本。新版《马克思恩格斯选集》第1—4卷，是中央编译局在原版基础上，根据《马克思恩格斯全集》俄文版和德文版的新版本译校而成，内容有一些调整。新版《马克思恩格斯选集》第1卷1843—1859年的著作，包括《雾月十八日》。③ 相比于《马克思恩格斯全集》第二版所收录的《雾月十八日》，《马克思恩格斯选集》第二版增添了马克思所撰写的《1869年第二版序言》和恩格斯所写的《1885年第二版的序言》。

2001年，中央编译局编译出版了《雾月十八日》的单行本，④ 又根据党中央实施马克思主义理论研究和建设工程规划的新要求，着手编辑了10卷本的《马克思恩格斯文集》，其中第2卷收录了《雾月十八日》一书，这是《雾月十八日》最新的版本。

（本文来自2013年中央编译出版社出版的白云真所著《马克思〈路易·波拿巴的雾月十八日〉研究读本》有关内容。）

---

① 中央编译局研究员张奇方先生在审读文稿时指出了添加意大利文、西班牙文的批注，深表谢意。
② 《马克思恩格斯全集》第11卷，北京：人民出版社1995年版。
③ 《马克思恩格斯选集》第1卷，北京：人民出版社1995年版。
④ 〔德〕马克思：《路易·波拿巴的雾月十八日》，中央编译局译，北京：人民出版社2001年版。

THE EIGHTEENTH BRUMAIRE OF LOUIS BONAPARTE

The Eighteenth Brumaire of Louis Bonaparte

By
KARL MARX

With Explanatory Notes

INTERNATIONAL PUBLISHERS
381 FOURTH AVENUE   NEW YORK

Edited by C. P. Dutt

All Rights Reserved

First published by Co-Operative Publishing Society
of Foreign Workers in the U.S.S.R.

Printed in the Union of Soviet Socialist Republics
Glavlit: B—78,307

CONTENTS

	Page
Author's Preface to the Second Edition	7
Frederick Engels' Preface to the Third German Edition	9
The Eighteenth Brumaire of Louis Bonaparte	13
II	23
III	36
IV	52
V	63
VI	82
VII	103
Explanatory Notes	123

AUTHOR'S PREFACE TO THE SECOND EDITION

My friend *Joseph Weydemeyer*,* whose death was so untimely, intended to publish a political weekly in New York from January 1, 1852. He invited me to provide this weekly with the history of the *coup d'état*. Down to the middle of February, I accordingly wrote him weekly articles under the title: *The Eighteenth Brumaire of Louis Bonaparte*. Meanwhile Weydemeyer's original plan had fallen through. Instead, in the spring of 1852 he published a monthly, *Die Revolution*, the second number of which consists of my *Eighteenth Brumaire*. A few hundred copies of this found their way into Germany at that time, without, however, getting into the actual book trade. A German publisher of extremely radical pretensions, to whom I offered the sale of my book, was most virtuously horrified at a "presumption" so "contrary to the times."

From the above facts it will be seen that the present work took shape under the immediate pressure of events and its historical material does not extend beyond the month of February (1852). Its re-publication now is due in part to the demand of the book trade, in part to the urgent requests of my friends in Germany.

Of the writings dealing with the same subject and appearing approximately *at the same time* as mine, only two deserve notice: Victor Hugo's *Napoleon le Petit* ** and Proudhon's *Coup d'État*.

Victor Hugo confines himself to biting and witty invective against the responsible author of the *coup d'état*. The event itself appears in his work like a bolt from the blue. He sees in it only the violent act of a single individual. He does not notice that he makes this individual great instead of little by ascribing to him a personal power of initiative such as would be without parallel in world history. Proudhon, for his part, seeks to represent the

* Military commandant of the St. Louis district during the American Civil War. [*Note by Karl Marx.*]
** Napoleon the Little.—*Ed.*

PREFACE

coup d'état as the result of the antecedent historical development. Unnoticeably, however, the historical exposition of the *coup d'état* is transformed into an historical *apologia* for its hero. Thus he falls into the error of our so-called *objective* historians. I, on the contrary, demonstrate how the *class struggle* in France created circumstances and relationships that made it possible for a grotesque mediocrity to play a hero's part.

A revision of the present work would have robbed it of its peculiar colouring. Accordingly I have confined myself to mere correction of printer's errors and to striking out allusions now no longer intelligible.

The concluding sentence of my work: "But if the imperial mantle finally falls on the shoulders of Louis Bonaparte, the iron statue of Napoleon will crash from the top of the Vendôme Column," has already been fulfilled.[1]

Colonel Charras opened the attack on the Napoleon cult in his work on the campaign of 1815. Subsequently, and particularly in the last few years, French literature has made an end of the Napoleon legend with the weapons of historical research, of criticism, of satire and of wit. Outside France this violent breach with the traditional popular belief, this tremendous mental revolution, has been little noticed and still less understood.

Lastly, I hope that my work will contribute towards eliminating the stock phrase now current, particularly in Germany, of so-called *Caesarism*. In this superficial historical analogy the main point is forgotten, namely that in ancient Rome the class struggle took place only within a privileged minority, between the free rich and the free poor, while the great, productive mass of the population, the slaves, formed the purely passive pedestal for these combatants. People forget *Sismondi's* significant remark: The Roman proletariat lived at the expense of society, while modern society lives at the expense of the proletariat. With so complete a difference between the material, economic conditions of the ancient and the modern class struggles, the political figures they produce can likewise have no more in common with one another than the Archbishop of Canterbury has with the High Priest Samuel.

London, June 23, 1869.

FREDERICK ENGELS' PREFACE TO THE THIRD GERMAN EDITION *

THE fact that a new edition of *The Eighteenth Brumaire* has become necessary, thirty-three years after its first appearance, proves that even today this little work has lost none of its value.

It is in truth a work of genius. Immediately after the event that struck the political world like a thunderbolt from a blue sky, that was condemned by some with loud cries of moral indignation and accepted by others as salvation from the revolution and as punishment for its errors, but was only wondered at by all and understood by none—immediately after this event Marx came out with a concise, epigrammatic exposition that laid bare the whole course of French history since the February days in its inner interconnection, reduced the miracle of December the Second to a natural, necessary result of this interconnection and in so doing did not even need to treat the hero of the *coup d'état* otherwise than with the contempt he so well deserved. And with such a master hand was the picture drawn that every fresh disclosure since made has only provided fresh proofs of how faithfully it reflected reality. This eminent understanding of the living history of the day, this clear-sighted appreciation of events at the moment of happening, is indeed without parallel.

But for this, Marx's thorough knowledge of French history was also requisite. France is the land where, more than anywhere else, the historical class struggles were each time fought out to a decision, where, consequently, the changing political forms within which they occur and in which their results are summarised have likewise been stamped with the sharpest outlines. The centre of feudalism in the Middle Ages, the model country of centralised monarchy resting on estates since the Renaissance,[2] France has

* 1883.—*Ed.*

PREFACE

demolished feudalism in the Great Revolution and established the unalloyed rule of the bourgeoisie in a classical purity unequalled by any other European land. And the struggle of the upward striving proletariat against the ruling bourgeoisie also appeared here in an acute form unknown elsewhere. This was the reason why Marx not only studied the past history of France with special interest, but also followed her current history in every detail, stored up the material for future use and consequently was never taken by surprise by the events.

In addition, however, there was still another circumstance. It was precisely Marx who had first discovered the great law of motion of history, the law according to which all historical struggles, whether they proceed in the political, religious, philosophical or some other ideological domain, are in fact only the more or less clear expression of struggles of social classes, and that the existence and thereby the collisions, too, of these classes are in turn conditioned by the degree of development of their economic position, by the mode of their production and by the form of exchange resulting from it. This law, which has the same significance for history as the law of the transformation of energy has for natural science—this law gave him here, too, the key to understanding the history of the Second French Republic. He put his law to the test on these historical events, and even after thirty-three years we must still say that it has stood the test brilliantly.

FREDERICK ENGELS

THE EIGHTEENTH BRUMAIRE OF
LOUIS BONAPARTE

THE EIGHTEENTH BRUMAIRE OF LOUIS BONAPARTE

I

HEGEL remarks somewhere that all great, world-historical facts and personages occur, as it were, twice. He has forgotten to add: the first time as tragedy, the second as farce. Caussidière for Danton, Louis Blanc for Robespierre, the Mountain of 1848 to 1851 for the Mountain of 1793 to 1795, the Nephew for the Uncle. And the same caricature occurs in the circumstances in which the second edition of the Eighteenth Brumaire is taking place.[3]

Men make their own history, but they do not make it just as they please; they do not make it under circumstances chosen by themselves, but under circumstances directly found, given and transmitted from the past. The tradition of all the dead generations weighs like a nightmare on the brain of the living. And just when they seem engaged in revolutionising themselves and things, in creating something entirely new, precisely in such epochs of revolutionary crisis they anxiously conjure up the spirits of the past to their service and borrow from them names, battle slogans and costumes in order to present the new scene of world history in this time-honoured disguise and this borrowed language. Thus Luther donned the mask of the Apostle Paul, the Revolution of 1789 to 1814 draped itself alternately as the Roman Republic and the Roman Empire, and the Revolution of 1848 knew nothing better to do than to parody, in turn, 1789 and the revolutionary tradition of 1793 to 1795. In like manner the beginner who has learnt a new language always translates it back into his mother tongue, but he has assimilated the spirit of the new language and can produce freely in it only when he moves in it without remembering the old and forgets in it his ancestral tongue.

But closer consideration of this world-historical conjuring up of the dead reveals at once a salient difference. Camille Desmoul-

THE EIGHTEENTH BRUMAIRE

ins, Danton, Robespierre, Saint-Just, Napoleon, the heroes, as well as the parties and the masses of the old French Revolution, performed the task of their time in Roman costume and with Roman phrases, the task of releasing and setting up modern *bourgeois* society. The first ones knocked the feudal basis to pieces and mowed off the feudal heads which had grown from it. The other created inside France the conditions under which free competition could first be developed, the parcelled landed property exploited, the unfettered productive power of the nation employed, and outside the French borders he everywhere swept the feudal formations away, so far as was necessary to furnish bourgeois society in France with a suitable up-to-date environment on the European Continent. The new social formation once established, the antediluvian Colossuses disappeared and with them the resurrected Romans—the Brutuses, Gracchi, Publicolas, the tribunes, the senators and Caesar himself. Bourgeois society in its sober reality had begotten its true interpreters and mouthpieces in the Says, Cousins, Royer-Collards, Benjamin Constants and Guizots; its real military leaders sat behind the office desks, and the hog-headed Louis XVIII was its political chief. Wholly absorbed in the production of wealth and in the peaceful struggle of competition, it no longer comprehended that ghosts from the days of Rome had watched over its cradle. But unheroic as bourgeois society is, yet it had need of heroism, of sacrifice, of terror, of civil war and of national battles to bring it into being. And in the classically austere traditions of the Roman Republic its gladiators found the ideals and the art forms, the self-deceptions that they needed in order to conceal from themselves the bourgeois limitations of the content of their struggles and to keep their passion at the height of the great historical tragedy. Similarly, at another stage of development, a century earlier, Cromwell[4] and the English people had borrowed speech, passions and illusions from the Old Testament for their bourgeois revolution. When the real aim had been achieved, when the bourgeois transformation of English society had been accomplished, Locke supplanted Habakkuk.

OF LOUIS BONAPARTE

The awakening of the dead in those revolutions therefore served the purpose of glorifying the new struggles, not of parodying the old; of magnifying the given tasks in imagination, not of taking flight from their solution in reality; of finding once more the spirit of revolution, not of making its ghost walk again.

From 1848 to 1851 only the ghost of the old Revolution walked, from Marrast, the *Republicain en gants jaunes*,* who disguised himself as the old Bailly, to the adventurer who hides his trivially repulsive features under the iron death mask of Napoleon. An entire people, which had imagined that by a revolution it had increased its power of action, suddenly finds itself set back into a dead epoch and, in order that no doubt as to the relapse may be possible, the old data again arise, the old chronology, the old names, the old edicts, which have long become a subject of antiquarian erudition, and the old henchmen, who had long seemed dead and decayed. The nation appears to itself like that mad Englishman in Bedlam, who fancies that he lives in the times of the ancient Pharaohs and daily bemoans the hard labour that he must perform in the Ethiopian mines as a gold digger, immured in this subterranean prison, a dimly burning lamp fastened to his head, the overseer of the slaves behind him with a long whip, and at the exits a confused mass of barbarian mercenaries, who understand neither the forced labourers in the mines nor one another, since they have no common speech. "And all this is expected of me," groans the mad Englishman, "of me, a free-born Briton, in order to make gold for the old Pharaohs." "In order to pay the debts of the Bonaparte family," sighs the French nation. The Englishman, so long as he was in his right mind, could not get rid of the fixed idea of making gold. The French, so long as they were engaged in revolution, could not get rid of the memory of Napoleon, as the election of December 10, 1848 ** proved. From the perils of revolution their longings went back to the flesh-pots of Egypt, and December 2, 1851, was the answer. They have not only a caricature of the old Napoleon, they have the old Napoleon himself,

---

* Republican in yellow gloves.—*Ed.*
** The day Louis Bonaparte was elected president of the republic.—*Ed.*

THE EIGHTEENTH BRUMAIRE

caricatured as he would inevitably appear in the middle of the nineteenth century.

The social revolution of the nineteenth century cannot draw its poetry from the past, but only from the future. It cannot begin with itself, before it has stripped off all superstition in regard to the past. Earlier revolutions required world-historical recollections in order to drug themselves concerning their own content. In order to arrive at its own content, the revolution of the nineteenth century must let the dead bury their dead. There the phrase went beyond the content; here the content goes beyond the phrase.

The February Revolution was a sudden attack, a taking of the old society by *surprise,* and the people proclaimed this unhoped for *stroke* as a world-historical deed, opening the new epoch. On December 2 the February Revolution is conjured away by a card-sharper's trick, and what seems overthrown is no longer the monarchy; it is the liberal concessions that were wrung from it by century-long struggles. Instead of *society* having conquered a new content for itself, the *state* only appears to have returned to its oldest form, to the shamelessly simple domination of the sabre and the cowl. This is the answer to the *coup de main* * of February, 1848, given by the *coup de tête* ** of December, 1851. Easy come, easy go. Meanwhile the interval has not passed by unused. During the years 1848 to 1851 French society has made up, and that by an abbreviated, because revolutionary, method, for the studies and experiences which, in a regular, so to speak, text-book development would have had to precede the February Revolution, if the latter was to be more than a disturbance of the surface. Society now seems to have fallen back behind its point of departure; it has in truth first to create for itself the revolutionary point of departure, the situation, the relationships, the conditions, under which modern revolution alone becomes serious.

Bourgeois revolutions, like those of the eighteenth century, storm more swiftly from success to success; their dramatic effects outdo each other; men and things seem set in sparkling brilliants; ecstasy is the everyday spirit; but they are short lived; soon they

* Sudden stroke.—*Ed.*
** Bold stroke.—*Ed.*

have attained their zenith, and a long depression lays hold of society before it learns soberly to assimilate the results of its storm and stress period. Proletarian revolutions, on the other hand, like those of the nineteenth century, criticise themselves constantly, interrupt themselves continually in their own course, come back to the apparently accomplished in order to recommence it afresh, deride with unmerciful thoroughness the inadequacies, weaknesses and paltrinesses of their first attempts, seem to throw down their adversary only in order that he may draw new strength from the earth and rise again more gigantic before them, recoil ever and anon from the indefinite prodigiousness of their own aims, until the situation has been created which makes all turning back impossible, and the conditions themselves cry out:

> Hic Rhodus, hic salta! *
> Hier ist die Rose, hier tanze! **

For the rest, every fairly competent observer, even if he had not followed the course of French development step by step, must have had a presentiment that a terrible fiasco was in store for the revolution. It was enough to hear the self-complacent howl of victory with which Messieurs the Democrats congratulated each other on the gracious consequences of May 2, 1852.[5] In their minds May 2, 1852, had become a fixed idea, a dogma, like the day on which Christ should reappear and the millennium begin, in the minds of the Chiliasts.[6] As ever, weakness had taken refuge in a belief in miracles, had fancied the enemy overcome when he was only conjured away in imagination, and lost all understanding of the present in a passive glorification of the future that was in store for it and of the deeds it had *in petto*,*** but merely did not want to carry out as yet. Those heroes, who seek to disprove their demonstrated incapacity by mutually offering each other their sympathy and getting together in a crowd, had tied up their bundles, collected their laurel wreaths in advance and were just then engaged in discounting on the exchange market the re-

---

* Here is Rhodes, leap here!—*Ed.*
** Here is the rose, dance here!—*Ed.*
*** In reserve.—*Ed.*

THE EIGHTEENTH BRUMAIRE

publics *in partibus*,* for which they had already thoughtfully organised the government personnel with all the calm of their unassuming disposition. December 2 struck them like a thunderbolt from a clear sky, and the peoples that in epochs of pusillanimous depression gladly let their inward apprehension be drowned by the loudest bawlers will perchance have convinced themselves that the times are past when the cackle of geese could save the Capitol.⁷

The Constitution, the National Assembly, the dynastic parties,** the blue and the red republicans,*** the heroes of Africa,ˢ the thunder from the platform, the sheet lightning of the daily press, the entire literature, the political names and the intellectual reputations, the civil law and the penal code, the *liberté, égalité, fraternité* **** and the Second of May, 1852—all have vanished like a phantasmagoria before the spell of a man whom even his enemies do not make out to be a magician. Universal suffrage seems to have survived only for a moment, in order that with its own hand it may make its last will and testament before the eyes of all the world and declare in the name of the people itself: Everything that exists has this much worth that it will perish.

It is not enough to say, as the French do, that their nation has been taken by surprise. A nation and a woman are not forgiven the unguarded hour in which the first adventurer that came along could violate them. The riddle is not solved by such terms of speech, but merely formulated in another way. It remains to be explained how a nation of thirty-six millions can be surprised and delivered unresisting into captivity by three high class swindlers.

Let us recapitulate in their general outlines the phases that the French Revolution has gone through from February 24, 1848, to December 1851.

Three main periods are unmistakable: the *February period*; the *period of the Constitution of the Republic* or *of the Constituent*

---

* In foreign parts, *i.e.*, existing only on paper.—*Ed.*
** For these parties see p. 31 *et seq.*—*Ed.*
*** The blue (bourgeois) and the red (socialist) republican parties.—*Ed.*
**** Liberty, equality, fraternity.—*Ed.*

OF LOUIS BONAPARTE

National Assembly, May 4, 1848, to May 29, 1849; the *period of the Constitutional Republic* or *of the Legislative National Assembly,* May 29, 1849, to December 2, 1851.

The first period, from February 24, or the overthrow of Louis Philippe, to May 4, 1848, the meeting of the Constituent Assembly, the *February period* proper, may be described as the *prologue* of the Revolution. Its character was officially expressed in the fact that the government improvised by it declared itself to be *provisional* and, like the government, everything that was instigated, attempted or enunciated during this period, proclaimed itself to be *provisional.* Nothing and nobody ventured to lay claim to the right of existence and of real action. All the elements that had prepared or determined the Revolution, the dynastic opposition, the republican bourgeoisie, the democratic-republican petty bourgeoisie and the social-democratic workers, provisionally found their place in the February *government.*

It could not be otherwise. The February days originally intended an electoral reform, by which the circle of the politically privileged among the possessing class itself was to be widened and the exclusive domination of the aristocracy of finance overthrown. When it came to the actual conflict, however, when the people mounted the barricades, the National Guard maintained a passive attitude, the army offered no serious resistance and the monarchy ran away, the republic appeared to be a matter of course. Every party construed it in its own sense. Having been won by the proletariat by force of arms, the proletariat impressed its stamp on it and proclaimed it to be a *social republic.* There was thus indicated the general content of the modern revolution, which stood in most singular contradiction to everything that, with the material at hand, with the degree of education attained by the masses, under the given circumstances and relationships, could be immediately realised in practice. On the other hand, the claims of all the remaining elements that had participated in the February Revolution were recognised by the lion's share that they obtained in the government. In no period do we therefore find a more confused mixture of high-flown phrases and actual uncertainty and clumsiness, of more enthusiastic striving for innovation and more deeply

2*

THE EIGHTEENTH BRUMAIRE

rooted domination of the old routine, of more apparent harmony of the whole society and more profound estrangement of its elements. While the Paris proletariat still revelled in the vision of the wide prospects that had opened before it and indulged in seriously meant discussions on social problems, the old powers of society had grouped themselves, assembled, reflected and found an unexpected support in the mass of the nation, the peasants and petty bourgeois, who all at once stormed on to the political stage, after the barriers of the July monarchy had fallen.

The *second period*, from May 4, 1848, to the end of May 1849, is the period of the *constitution*, of the *foundation of the bourgeois republic*. Directly after the February days the dynastic opposition had not only been surprised by the republicans, the republicans by the socialists, but all France had been surprised by Paris. The National Assembly, which had met on May 4, 1848, having emerged from the national elections, represented the nation. It was a living protest against the presumptuous aspirations of the February days and was to reduce the results of the Revolution to the bourgeois scale. In vain the Paris proletariat, which immediately grasped the character of this National Assembly, attempted on May 15, a few days after it met, forcibly to deny its existence, to dissolve it, to disintegrate once more into its constituent parts the organic form in which the proletariat was threatened by the reactionary spirit of the nation. As is known, May 15 had no other result save that of removing Blanqui and his comrades, that is, the real leaders of the proletarian party, [the revolutionary communists] [9] from the public stage for the entire duration of the cycle we are considering.

The *bourgeois monarchy* of Louis Philippe can only be followed by the *bourgeois republic*, that is, if a limited section of the bourgeoisie formerly ruled in the name of the king, the whole of the bourgeoisie will now rule in the name of the people. The demands of the Paris proletariat are utopian nonsense to which an end must be put. To this declaration of the Constituent National Assembly the Paris proletariat replied with the *June Insurrection*, the most colossal event in the history of European civil wars. The bourgeois republic triumphed. On its side stood the

OF LOUIS BONAPARTE

aristocracy of finance, the industrial bourgeoisie, the middle class, the petty bourgeois, the army, the *lumpenproletariat* organised as the Mobile Guard,* the intellectual lights, the clergy, and the rural population. On the side of the Paris proletariat stood none but itself. More than three thousand insurgents were butchered after the victory, and fifteen thousand were transported without trial. With this defeat the proletariat passes into the background of the revolutionary stage. It attempts to press forward again on every occasion, as soon as the movement appears to make a fresh start, but with ever decreased expenditure of strength and always more insignificant results. As soon as one of the social strata situated above it gets into revolutionary ferment, it enters into an alliance with it and so shares all the defeats that the different parties suffer one after another. But these subsequent blows become steadily weaker, the more they are distributed over the entire surface of society. Its more important leaders in the Assembly and the press successively fall victims to the courts, and ever more equivocal figures come to the fore. In part it throws itself into *doctrinaire experiments, exchange banks and workers' associations, hence into a movement in which it renounces the revolutionising of the old world by means of its own great, combined resources, and seeks, rather, to achieve its salvation behind society's back, in private fashion, within its limited conditions of existence, and hence inevitably suffers shipwreck.* It seems to be unable either to rediscover revolutionary greatness in itself or to win new energy from the alliances newly entered into, until *all classes* with which it contended in June themselves lie prostrate beside it. But at least it succumbs with the honours of the great, world historical struggle; not only France, but all Europe trembles at the June earthquake, while the ensuing defeats of the upper classes are so cheaply bought that they require bare-faced exaggeration by the victorious party to be able to pass for events at all and become the more ignominious the further the defeated party is removed from the proletariat.

The defeat of the June insurgents, to be sure, had now pre-

* Marx gives a characterisation of the *Garde Mobile* in *The Class Struggles in France* (1848-1850).—Ed.

THE EIGHTEENTH BRUMAIRE

pared and levelled the ground on which the bourgeois republic could be founded and built up, but it had shown at the same time that in Europe there are other questions involved than that of "republic or monarchy." It had revealed that here *bourgeois republic* signifies the unlimited despotism of one class over other classes. It had proved that in lands with an old civilisation, with a developed formation of classes, with modern conditions of production and with an intellectual consciousness into which all traditional ideas had been dissolved by centuries of effort, *the republic* signifies *in general only the political form of the revolution of bourgeois society* and not its *conservative form of life*, as, for example, in the United States of North America, where, though classes, indeed, already exist, they have not yet become fixed, but continually change and interchange their elements in a constant state of flux, where the modern means of production, instead of coinciding with a stagnant surplus population, rather supply the relative deficiency of heads and hands and where, finally, the feverishly youthful movement of material production, that has a new world to make its own, has left neither time nor opportunity for abolishing the old spirit world.

During the June days all classes and parties had united in the *party of order* against the proletarian class as the *party of anarchy*, of socialism, of communism. They had "saved" society from *"the enemies of society."* They had given out the watchwords of the old society, *"property, family, religion, order,"* to their army as pass words and proclaimed to the counter-revolutionary crusaders: "In this sign you will conquer!" From that moment, as soon as one of the numerous parties which had gathered under this sign against the June insurgents seeks to hold the revolutionary battle field in its own class interests, it goes down before the cry: "Property, family, religion, order." Society is saved just as often as the circle of its rulers contracts, as a more exclusive interest is maintained against a wider one. Every demand of the simplest bourgeois financial reform, of the most ordinary liberalism, of the most formal republicanism, of the most insipid democracy, is simultaneously castigated as an "attempt on society" and stigmatised as "socialism." And, finally, the high priests of "religion and order" themselves are driven with kicks from their Pythian tripods, hauled out of their beds in the darkness of night, put in prison-vans, thrown into dungeons or sent into exile; their temple is razed to the ground, their mouths are sealed, their pens broken, their law torn to pieces in the name of religion, of property, of family, of order. Bourgeois fanatics for order are shot down on their balconies by mobs of drunken soldiers, their domestic sanctuaries profaned, their houses bombarded for amusement— in the name of property, of family, of religion and of order. Finally the scum of bourgeois society forms *the holy phalanx of order* and the hero Crapulinsky [10] installs himself in the Tuileries * as the *"saviour of society."*

II

Let us pick up the threads of the development once more.

The history of the *Constituent National Assembly* since the June days is the *history of the domination and the liquidation of the republican section of the bourgeoisie,* of that section which is known by the names of tricolour republicans, pure republicans, political republicans, formalist republicans, etc.

Under the bourgeois monarchy of Louis Philippe it had formed the *official* republican *opposition* and consequently a recognised, component part of the political world of the day. It had its representatives in the Chambers and a considerable sphere of influence in the press. Its Paris organ, the *National,* was considered just as respectable in its way as the *Journal des Débats.* Its character corresponded to this position under the constitutional monarchy. It was not a section of the bourgeoisie held together by great, common interests and marked off by specific conditions of production. It was a coterie of republican-minded bourgeois—writers, lawyers, officers and officials—that owed its influence to the personal antipathies of the country to Louis Philippe, to memories of the old republic, to the republican faith of a number of enthusiasts, above all, however, to *French nationalism,* whose hatred

---

* The residence of the head of the government in France.—*Ed.*

THE EIGHTEENTH BRUMAIRE

of the Vienna treaties and of the alliance with England it stirred up perpetually. A large part of the following that the *National* had under Louis Philippe was due to this concealed imperialism, which could consequently confront it later, under the republic, as a deadly rival in the person of Louis Bonaparte. It fought the aristocracy of finance, as did all the rest of the bourgeois opposition. Polemics against the budget, which were closely connected in France with fighting the aristocracy of finance, procured popularity too cheaply, and material for puritanical leading articles too plentifully, not to be exploited. The industrial bourgeoisie was grateful to it for its slavish defence of the French protectionist system, which it accepted, however, more on national grounds than on grounds of political economy; the bourgeoisie as a whole was grateful to it for its vicious denunciation of communism and socialism. For the rest, the party of the *National* was purely republican, that is, it demanded a republican instead of a monarchist form of bourgeois rule and, above all, the lion's share of this rule. Concerning the conditions of this transformation it was by no means clear. On the other hand, what was clear as daylight to it and was publicly acknowledged at the reform banquets in the last days of Louis Philippe, was its unpopularity with the democratic petty bourgeois and, in particular, with the revolutionary proletariat. These pure republicans, as is, indeed, the way with pure republicans, were already on the point of contenting themselves in the first instance with a regency of the Duchess of Orleans,[11] when the February Revolution broke out and assigned their best known representatives a place in the Provisional Government. From the start, they naturally had the confidence of the bourgeoisie and a majority in the Constituent National Assembly. The *Socialist* elements of the Provisional Government were excluded forthwith from the Executive Commission which the National Assembly formed when it met, and the party of the *National* took advantage of the outbreak of the June Insurrection to discharge the *Executive Commission* also, and therewith to get rid of its immediate rivals, the *petty-bourgeois* or *democratic republicans* (Ledru-Rollin, etc). Cavaignac, the general of the bourgeois-republican party, who commanded the June battle, took the place of the Executive Commission with a sort of dictatorial power. Marrast, former editor in chief of the *National*, became the perpetual president of the Constituent Assembly, and the ministries, as well as all other important posts, fell to the portion of the pure republicans.

The republican bourgeois section, which had long regarded itself as the legitimate heir of the July monarchy, thus found itself successful beyond its hopes; it attained power, however, not as it had dreamed under Louis Philippe, through a liberal revolt of the bourgeoisie against the throne, but through a rising of the proletariat against capital, a rising laid low with grape-shot. What it had pictured to itself as the *most revolutionary* happening, turned out in reality to be the *most counter-revolutionary*. The fruit fell into its lap, but it fell from the tree of knowledge, not from the tree of life.

The exclusive *rule of the bourgeois republicans lasted* only from June 24 to December 10, 1848. It is summed up in the *drafting of a republican Constitution* and in the *state of siege of Paris*.

The new *Constitution* was at bottom only the republicanised edition of the constitutional Charter of 1830.[12] The narrow electoral qualification of the July monarchy, which even excluded a large part of the bourgeoisie from political rule, was incompatible with the existence of the bourgeois republic. In lieu of this qualification, the February Revolution had at once proclaimed direct, universal suffrage. The bourgeois republicans could not revoke this event. They had to content themselves with adding the limiting proviso of a six months' domicile in the constituency. The old organisation of government, of the municipal system, of the administration of law, of the army, etc., continued to exist inviolate, or, where the Constitution changed them, the change concerned the table of contents, not the contents; the name, not the thing.

The inevitable general staff of the liberties of 1848, personal liberty, liberty of the press, of speech, of association, of assembly, of education and of religion, etc., received a constitutional uniform, which made them invulnerable. Each of these liberties, namely, is proclaimed as the *absolute* right of the French *citoyen*,*

---

* Citizen.—*Ed.*

THE EIGHTEENTH BRUMAIRE

but always with the marginal note that it is unlimited so far as it is not restricted by the *"equal rights of others* and the *public safety"* or by "laws" which are intended to secure just this harmony of the individual liberties with one another and with the public safety. For example: "The citizens have the right of association, of peaceful and unarmed assembly, of petition and of the free expression of opinions, whether in the press or otherwise. *The enjoyment of these rights has no limit save the equal rights of others and the public safety.*" (Chapter II of the French Constitution, § 8.)—"Education is free. Freedom of education shall be *enjoyed* under the conditions fixed by law and under the general supervision of the state." (*Ibidem*, § 9.)—"The domicile of every citizen is inviolable *except* in the forms prescribed by law." (Chapter I, § 3.) Etc., etc.—The Constitution, therefore, constantly refers to future *organic* laws, which are to put into effect those marginal notes and regulate the enjoyment of these unrestricted liberties so that they collide neither with one another nor with the public safety. And later, the organic laws were brought into being by the friends of order and all those liberties regulated in such a way that the bourgeoisie in its enjoyment of them does not come into collision with the equal rights of the other classes. Where it forbids these liberties entirely to "the others" or permits enjoyment of them under conditions that are just so many police traps, this always happened solely in the interest of the "public safety," that is, the safety of the bourgeoisie, as the Constitution prescribes. In the sequel, both sides accordingly appeal with complete justice to the Constitution, the friends of order, who suspended all these liberties, as well as the democrats, who demanded them back. Each paragraph of the Constitution, namely, contains in itself its own antithesis, its own Upper and Lower House, namely liberty in the general phrase, suspension of liberty in the marginal note. So long, therefore, as the *name* of freedom was respected and only its actual realisation prevented, of course in a legal way, the constitutional existence of liberty remained intact and inviolate, however mortal the blows dealt to its *everyday* existence.

OF LOUIS BONAPARTE

This Constitution, made inviolable in so ingenious a manner, was nevertheless, like Achilles, vulnerable in one point, not in the heel, but in the head, or rather in the two heads in which it issued—the *Legislative Assembly,* on the one hand, the *President,* on the other. Glance through the Constitution and you will find that only the paragraphs in which the relationship of the President to the Legislative Assembly is determined are absolute, positive, non-contradictory, incapable of distortion. Here, that is to say, the issue for the bourgeois republicans was to safeguard themselves. Paragraphs 45-70 of the Constitution are so worded that the National Assembly can remove the President constitutionally, whereas the President can only remove the National Assembly unconstitutionally, only by setting aside the Constitution itself. Here, therefore, it challenges its overthrow by force. It not only sanctifies the division of powers, like the Charter of 1830, it widens it into an intolerable contradiction. *The play of the constitutional powers,* as Guizot termed the parliamentary squabble between the legislative and executive authorities, is in the Constitution of 1848 continually played *va-banque.** On one side are seven hundred and fifty representatives of the people, elected by universal suffrage and eligible for re-election; they form an uncontrollable, indissoluble, indivisible National Assembly, a National Assembly that enjoys legislative omnipotence, decides in the last instance on war, peace and commercial treaties, alone possesses the right of amnesty and, by its permanence, perpetually holds the front of the stage. On the other side is the President, with all the attributes of royal power, with authority to appoint and dismiss his ministers independently of the National Assembly, with all the resources of the executive power in his hands, bestowing all posts and disposing thereby in France over at least a million and a half existences, for so many depend on the five hundred thousand officials and the officers of every rank. He has the whole of the armed forces behind him. He enjoys the privilege of pardoning individual criminals, of suspending National Guards, of discharging, in agreement with the Council of State, the general, cantonal

---

* Staking all on one hazard.—*Ed.*

THE EIGHTEENTH BRUMAIRE

and municipal councils elected by the citizens themselves. Initiative and direction are reserved to him in all treaties with foreign countries. While the Assembly constantly performs on the boards and is exposed to the searching light of day, he leads a hidden life in the Elysian fields, and that with Article 45 of the Constitution before his eyes and in his heart, crying to him daily: *"Frère, il faut mourir!"** Your power ceases on the second Sunday of the lovely month of May in the fourth year after your election! Then the glory is at an end, the piece is not played twice and if you have debts, look to it betimes that you pay them off with the six hundred thousand francs granted you by the Constitution, unless, perchance, you should prefer to go to Clichy ** on the second Monday of the lovely month of May!—Thus, if the Constitution assigns actual power to the President, it seeks to secure moral power for the National Assembly. Apart from the fact that it is impossible to create a moral power by paragraphs of law, the Constitution here suspends itself once more, by having the President elected by all Frenchmen through direct suffrage. While the votes of France are split up among the seven hundred and fifty members of the National Assembly, they are, on the contrary, here concentrated on a single individual. While each separate representative of the people represents only this or that party, this or that town, this or that bridge-head, or even the mere necessity of electing one of the seven hundred and fifty, in which neither the cause nor the man is closely examined, the President is the elect of the nation and the act of his election is the trump that the sovereign people plays once every four years. The elected National Assembly stands in a metaphysical relation, but the elected President in a personal relation to the nation. The National Assembly indeed, exhibits in its individual representatives the manifold aspects of the national spirit, but in the President this national spirit finds its incarnation. As against the Assembly, he possesses a sort of divine right, he is President, by grace of the people.

Thetis, the sea goddess, had prophesied to Achilles that he

* Brother you must die!—*Ed.*
** The debtors' prison in Paris.—*Ed.*

would die in the bloom of youth. The Constitution, which, like Achilles, had its weak spot, had also, like Achilles, its presentiment that it must go to an early death. It was sufficient for the constitution-making, pure republicans to cast a glance from the cloud-kingdom of their ideal republic at the profane world, in order to perceive how the arrogance of the royalists, the Bonapartists, the democrats, the communists as well as their own discredit grew daily in the same measure as they approached the completion of their great legislative work of art, without Thetis on this account having to leave the sea and communicate the secret to them. They sought to cheat destiny by constitutional cunning, through § III of the Constitution, according to which every motion for the *revision of the Constitution* must have at least three-quarters of the votes cast for it in three successive debates between which an entire month must always lie, with the added proviso that not less than five hundred members of the National Assembly must vote. Thereby they merely made the impotent attempt to exercise as a parliamentary minority, as which they already saw themselves prophetically in their mind's eye, a power which at the moment when they commanded a parliamentary majority and all the resources of governmental authority was slipping daily more and more from their feeble hands.

Finally the Constitution, in a melodramatic paragraph, entrusts itself "to the vigilance and the patriotism of the whole French people and every single Frenchman," after it had previously entrusted the "vigilant" and "patriotic" in another paragraph to the tender, painstaking care of the High Court of Justice, of the *"haute cour,"* established by it for the purpose.

Such was the Constitution of 1848, which on December 2, 1851, was overthrown not by a head, but fell at the touch of a mere hat; this hat, to be sure, was a three-cornered, Napoleonic hat.

While the bourgeois republicans in the Assembly were busy elaborating, discussing and voting this Constitution, outside the Assembly Cavaignac maintained the *state of siege of Paris*. The state of siege of Paris was the *accoucheur* * of the Constituent Assembly in its travail of republican creation. If the Constitution is

* Midwife.—*Ed.*

THE EIGHTEENTH BRUMAIRE

subsequently put out of existence by bayonets, it must not be forgotten that it was likewise by bayonets, and these turned against the people, that it had to be protected in its mother's womb and by bayonets that it had to be brought into existence. The forefathers of the "honest republicans" had sent their symbol, the tricolour, on a tour round Europe. They now, in turn, also produced an invention that made its way by itself over the whole continent, but returned to France with ever renewed love until it has now acquired citizen rights in half her departments—*the state of siege*. It was a splendid invention, periodically employed in every ensuing crisis in the course of the French Revolution. But barrack and bivouac, which were periodically laid on French society's head to compress its brain and make a quiet man of it; sabre and musket, which were periodically allowed to direct and administer, hold in tutelage and act as censor, play policeman and do nightwatchman's duties; moustache and uniform, which were periodically trumpeted as the highest wisdom and master of society—were not barrack and bivouac, sabre and musket, moustache and uniform, finally bound to hit upon the idea of saving society, rather, once and for all, by proclaiming their own regime as the highest and freeing bourgeois society from all the trouble of governing itself? Barrack and bivouac, sabre and musket, moustache and uniform, were bound to hit upon the idea all the more as they might then also expect better cash payment for their higher services, whereas from the merely periodical state of siege and the transient savings of society at the bidding of this or that bourgeois faction they gained little of substance beyond some killed and wounded and some friendly bourgeois grimaces. Should not the military, at length, likewise one day play the state of siege in their own interest and for their own interest and at the same time besiege the bourgeois *bourses?* Moreover, be it remarked in passing, one must not forget that *Colonel Bernard,* the same president of the military commission who under Cavaignac had 15,000 insurgents deported without trial, is at this moment again at the head of the military commissions active in Paris.

If, with the state of siege in Paris, the honest, the pure republicans founded the nursery in which the prætorians [13] of Decem-

OF LOUIS BONAPARTE

ber 2, 1851, were to grow up, on the other hand they deserve praise for the reason that, instead of exaggerating the national sentiment as under Louis Philippe, they now, when they have command of the national power, crawl before foreign countries, and, instead of setting Italy free, let her be reconquered by Austrians and Neapolitans. Louis Bonaparte's election as president on December 10, 1848, put an end to the dictatorship of Cavaignac and the Constituent Assembly.

In § 44 of the Constitution it is stated: "The President of the French Republic must never have lost his status as a French citizen." The first President of the French Republic, L. N. Bonaparte, had not merely lost his status as a French citizen, had not only been an English special constable, he was even a naturalised Swiss.

I have worked out elsewhere the significance of the election of December 10. I will not revert to it here. It is sufficient to remark here that it was a *reaction of the peasants*, who had had to pay the costs of the February Revolution, against the remaining classes of the nation, a *reaction of the countryside against the town*. It met with great approval in the army, for which the republicans of the *National* had provided neither glory nor additional pay, among the big bourgeoisie, which hailed Bonaparte as a bridge to monarchy; among the proletarians and petty bourgeois, who hailed him as a scourge for Cavaignac. I shall have an opportunity later of going more closely into the relationship of the peasants to the French Revolution.

The period from December 20, 1848,[14] until the dissolution of the Constituent Assembly in May, 1849, comprises the history of the downfall of the bourgeois republicans. After having founded a republic for the bourgeoisie, driven the revolutionary proletariat out of the field and reduced the democratic petty bourgeoisie to silence for the time being, they are themselves thrust aside by the mass of the bourgeoisie, which justly impounds this republic as *its property*. This bourgeois mass was, however, *royalist*. One section of it, the large landowners, had ruled during the *Restoration*[15] and was accordingly *Legitimist*. The other, the aristocrats of finance and big industrialists, had ruled during the July Monarchy

THE EIGHTEENTH BRUMAIRE

and was consequently *Orleanist*. The high dignitaries of the army, the university, the church, the bar, the academy and the press were to be found on either side, though in different proportions. Here in the bourgeois republic, which bore neither the name *Bourbon* nor the name *Orleans*, but the name *capital*, they had found the form of state in which they could rule *conjointly*. The June Insurrection had already united them in the "Party of Order." Now it was necessary, in the first place, to remove the coterie of bourgeois republicans, who still occupied seats in the National Assembly. Just as these pure republicans were brutal in their misuse of physical force against the people, to the same degree were they now cowardly, downcast, broken-spirited and incapable of fighting in their retreat when it was a question of maintaining their republicanism and their legislative rights against the executive power and the royalists. I do not have to relate here the ignominious story of their dissolution. They were not destroyed; they passed away. Their history has come to an end forever, and, both inside and outside the Assembly, they figure in the following period only as memories, memories that again seem to become living whenever the mere name, republic, is once more the issue and as often as the revolutionary conflict threatens to sink down to the lowest level. I may remark in passing that the journal which gave its name to this party, the *National*, went over to socialism in the following period.

Before we finish with this period we must still cast a retrospective glance at the two powers, one of which annihilates the other on December 2, 1851, whereas from December 10, 1848, until the exit of the Constituent Assembly they lived in conjugal relations. We mean Louis Bonaparte, on the one hand, and the party of the royalist coalition, the Party of Order, of the big bourgeoisie, on the other. On his entry into the presidency, Bonaparte at once formed a ministry of the Party of Order, at the head of which he placed Odilon Barrot, the old leader, *nota bene*, of the most liberal section of the parliamentary bourgeoisie. M. Barrot had at last secured the portfolio, the spectre of which had haunted him since 1830, and what is more, the premiership in the ministry;

OF LOUIS BONAPARTE

but not, as he had imagined under Louis Philippe, as the most advanced leader of the parliamentary opposition, but with the task of killing a parliament, and as the confederate of all his arch-enemies, Jesuits and Legitimists. At length he brings the bride home, but only after she has become a prostitute. Bonaparte appeared to efface himself completely. This party acted for him.

The first council of ministers at once resolved on the expedition to Rome, which they agreed to undertake behind the back of the National Assembly and the means for which they agreed to obtain from it by false pretences. Thus they began by swindling the National Assembly and secretly conspiring with the absolutist powers abroad against the revolutionary Roman republic. In the same manner and with the same manœuvres Bonaparte prepared his coup of December 2 against the royalist Legislative Assembly and its constitutional republic. Let us not forget that the same party which formed Bonaparte's ministry on December 20, 1848, formed the majority of the Legislative National Assembly on December 2, 1851.

In August the Constituent Assembly had decided to dissolve only after it had worked out and promulgated a whole series of organic laws that were to supplement the Constitution. On January 6, 1849, the Party of Order had a deputy named Rateau move that it should let the organic laws go and, rather, decide on its *own dissolution.* Not merely the ministry, with Odilon Barrot at its head, but the whole of the royalist members of the National Assembly bullyingly told it at this moment that its dissolution was necessary for the restoration of credit, for the consolidation of order, for putting an end to the indefinite provisional arrangements and for establishing a definite state of affairs; that it hampered the productivity of the new government and sought to prolong its existence merely out of malice; that the country was tired of it. Bonaparte took note of all this invective against the legislative power, learnt it by heart and proved to the parliamentary royalists on December 2, 1851, that he had learnt from them. He reiterated their own catchwords against them.

The Barrot ministry and the Party of Order went further. They caused *petitions to the National Assembly* to be made throughout

3 K. Marx, The 18th Brumaire

THE EIGHTEENTH BRUMAIRE

France, in which this body was most politely requested to disappear. Against the National Assembly, the constitutionally organised expression of the people, they thus led its unorganised masses into fire. They taught Bonaparte to appeal from the parliamentary assemblies to the people. At length, on January 29, the day had come on which the Constituent Assembly was to decide concerning its own dissolution. The National Assembly found the building where its sessions were held occupied by the military; Changarnier, the general of the Party of Order, in whose hands the supreme command of the National Guard and troops of the line had been united, held a great review in Paris, as if a battle were impending, and the royalists in coalition threateningly declared to the Constituent Assembly that force would be employed if it were not docile. It was docile and only bargained for a short extra term of life. What was January 29 but the *coup d'état* of December 2, 1851, only carried out by the royalists with Bonaparte against the republican National Assembly? The gentlemen did not observe or did not wish to observe that Bonaparte availed himself of January 29, 1849, to have a portion of the troops march past him in front of the Tuileries and seized with avidity on just this first public calling out of the military power against the parliamentary power to foreshadow Caligula.[16] They, to be sure, saw only their Changarnier.

One motive, in particular, that actuated the Party of Order in forcibly cutting short the duration of the Constituent Assembly's life consisted in the *organic* laws supplementing the Constitution, such as the education law, the law on religious worship, etc. To the royalists in coalition it was most important that they should make these laws themselves and not let them be made by the republicans, who had grown mistrustful. Among these organic laws, however, was also a law on the responsibility of the President of the Republic. In 1851 the Legislative Assembly was occupied with the drafting of just such a law, when Bonaparte anticipated this coup with the coup of December 2. In their parliamentary winter campaign of 1851 what would the royalists in coalition not have given to have found the Responsibility Law ready to hand, and drawn up, at that, by a mistrustful malicious republican Assembly!

OF LOUIS BONAPARTE

After the Constituent Assembly had itself shattered its last weapon on January 29, 1849, the Barrot ministry and the friends of order hounded it to death, left nothing undone that could humiliate it and wrested from its self-despairing weakness laws that cost it the last remnant of respect in the eyes of the public. Bonaparte, occupied with his fixed Napoleonic idea, was bold enough to exploit publicly this degradation of the parliamentary power. That is to say, when on May 8, 1849, the National Assembly passed a vote of censure on the ministry because of the occupation of Civita Vecchia by Oudinot, and ordered it to bring back the Roman expedition to its ostensible purpose, Bonaparte published the same evening in the *Moniteur* a letter to Oudinot, in which he congratulated him on his heroic exploits and, in contrast to the ink-slinging parliamentarians, already posed as the generous protector of the army. The royalists smiled at this. They regarded him simply as their dupe. Finally, when Marrast, the President of the Constituent Assembly, believed for a moment that the safety of the National Assembly was endangered and, relying on the Constitution, requisitioned a colonel and his regiment, the colonel declined, took refuge in discipline and referred Marrast to Changarnier, who scornfully refused him with the remark that he did not like *baionettes intelligentes*.* In November, 1851, when the royalists in coalition wished to begin the decisive struggle with Bonaparte, they sought to push through in their notorious *Queastors' Bill* [17] the principle of the direct requisition of troops by the President of the National Assembly. One of their generals, Leflô, had signed the bill. In vain did Changarnier vote for it and Thiers pay homage to the far-sighted wisdom of the former Constituent Assembly. The *War Minister, Saint-Arnaud,* answered him as Changarnier had answered Marrast—and to the acclamation of the Mountain!

Thus the *Party of Order*, when it was not yet the National Assembly, when it was still only the ministry, had itself stigmatised the *parliamentary regime*. And it makes an outcry when December 2, 1851, banished this regime from France!

---

* Intelligent bayonets.—*Ed.*

THE EIGHTEENTH BRUMAIRE

We wish it a happy journey.

III

On May 29, 1849, the Legislative National Assembly met. On December 2, 1851, it was forcibly dissolved. This period covers the life of the *constitutional or parliamentary republic.*

[It is subdivided into three main periods: *May 29, 1849, to June 13, 1849,* struggle of the democracy and the bourgeoisie, *defeat of the petty-bourgeois or democratic party; June 13, 1849, to May 31, 1850,* parliamentary dictatorship of the bourgeoisie, that is, of the Orleanists and Legitimists in coalition or the Party of Order, dictatorship that is completed by the *abolition of universal suffrage; May 31, 1850, up to December 2, 1851,* struggle of the bourgeoisie and Bonaparte, *overthrow of bourgeois rule, downfall of the constitutional or parliamentary republic.*]*

In the first French Revolution the rule of the *Constitutionalists* is followed by the rule of the *Girondins* and the rule of the *Girondins* by the rule of the *Jacobins.* Each of these parties supported itself on the more progressive party. As soon as it has brought the revolution far enough to be unable to follow it further, still less to go ahead of it, it is thrust aside by the bolder ally that stands behind it and sent to the guillotine. The revolution thus moves along an ascending line.

It is the reverse with the Revolution of 1848. The proletarian party appears as an appendage of the petty-bourgeois democratic party. It is betrayed and dropped by the latter on April 16, May 15, and in the June days. The democratic party, in its turn, leans on the shoulders of the bourgeois-republican party. The bourgeois-republicans no sooner believe themselves well established than they shake off the troublesome comrade and support themselves on the shoulders of the Party of Order. The Party of Order hunches its shoulders, lets the bourgeois-republicans tumble and throws itself on the shoulders of armed force. It fancies it is still sitting on its shoulders when, one fine morning, it perceives that the shoulders have transformed themselves into bayonets. Each

---

* This paragraph was omitted in the third German edition (1883).—*Ed.*

OF LOUIS BONAPARTE

party strikes from behind at that pressing further and leans from in front on that pressing back. No wonder that in this ridiculous posture it loses its balance and, having made the inevitable grimaces, collapses with curious capers. The revolution thus moves in a descending line. It finds itself in this state of retrogressive motion before the last February barricade has been cleared away and the first revolutionary authority constituted.

The period that we have before us comprises the most motley mixture of crying contradictions: constitutionalists who conspire openly against the Constitution; revolutionaries who are confessedly constitutional; a National Assembly that wants to be omnipotent and always remains parliamentary; a Mountain that finds its vocation in patience and counters its present defeats by prophesying future victories; royalists who form the *patres conscripti* * of the republic and are forced by the situation to keep the hostile royal houses, to which they adhere, abroad, and the republic, which they hate, in France; an executive power that finds its strength in its very weakness and its respectability in the contempt that it calls forth; a republic that is nothing but the combined infamy of two monarchies, the Restoration and the July Monarchy, with an imperial label—combinations, whose first proviso is separation; struggles, whose first law is indecision; wild, empty agitation in the name of peace, most solemn preaching of peace in the name of revolution; passions without truth, truth without passion; heroes without heroic deeds, history without events; development, whose sole driving force seems to be the calendar, wearying with constant repetition of the same tensions and relaxations; antagonisms, that periodically seem to reach a high pitch only in order to lose their acuteness and fall away without being able to find a solution; pretentiously paraded exertions and bourgeois terror at the danger of the end of the world and at the same time the pettiest intrigues and court comedies played by the world redeemers, who in their *laisser aller* ** remind us less of the Day of Judgment than of the times of the Fronde [18]—the

---

* *Conscript fathers.* In ancient Rome every Senator began his speech to the Senate with this appellation.—*Ed.*
** Letting things take their course.—*Ed.*

THE EIGHTEENTH BRUMAIRE

official collective genius of France brought to naught by the artful stupidity of a single individual; the collective will of the nation, as often as it speaks through universal suffrage, seeking its appropriate expression through the ancient enemies of the mass interests, until at length it finds it in the self-will of a filibuster. If any section of history has been painted grey on grey, it is this. Men and events appear inverted Schlemihls,[19] as shadows that have lost their substance. The revolution itself paralyses its own bearers and endows only its adversaries with passionate forcefulness. When the "red spectre," continually conjured up and exorcised by the counter-revolutionaries, finally appears, it appears not with the Phrygian cap of anarchy on its head, but in the uniform of order, in *red breeches*.

We have seen that the ministry which Bonaparte installed on December 20, 1848, on his Ascension Day, was a ministry of the Party of Order, of the Legitimist and Orleanist coalition. This Barrot-Falloux ministry had outlived the republican Constituent Assembly, whose term of life it had more or less violently cut short, and found itself still at the helm. Changarnier, the general of the allied royalists, continued to unite in his person the general command of the first division of the army and the National Guard of Paris. The general elections had finally secured the Party of Order a large majority in the National Assembly. Here the deputies and peers of Louis Philippe encountered a hallowed host of Legitimists, for whom numerous ballot papers of the nation had become transformed into admission cards to the political stage. The Bonapartist representatives of the people were too few to be able to form an independent parliamentary party. They appear merely as the *mauvaise queue* * of the Party of Order. Thus the Party of Order was in possession of the governmental power, the army and the legislative body, in short, of the whole power of the state, while it had been morally strengthened by the general elections, which made its rule appear as the will of the people, and by the simultaneous triumph of counter-revolution over the whole continent of Europe.[20]

---

* Evil appendage.—*Ed.*

OF LOUIS BONAPARTE

Never did a party open its compaign with greater resources or under more favourable auspices.

The shipwrecked *pure republicans* found themselves reduced to a clique of some fifty men in the National Assembly, the African generals—Cavaignac, Lamorcière and Bedeau—at their head. The great opposition party, however, was formed by the *Mountain*. The *Social Democratic* Party had given itself this parliamentary name. It commanded more than two hundred of the seven hundred and fifty votes of the National Assembly and was consequently at least as powerful as any one of the three factions of the Party of Order taken by itself. Its relative minority compared with the entire royalist coalition seemed compensated by special circumstances. Not only did the elections in the departments show that it had gained a considerable following among the rural population. It counted in its ranks almost all the deputies from Paris; the army had made a confession of democratic faith by the election of three non-commissioned officers, and the leader of the Mountain, Ledru-Rollin, in contradistinction to all the representatives of the Party of Order, had been raised to the parliamentary peerage by five departments, which had pooled their votes for him. In view of the inevitable clashes of the royalists among themselves and of the whole Party of Order with Bonaparte, the Mountain seemed to have all the elements of success before it on May 29, 1849. A fortnight later it had lost everything, honour included.

Before we pursue parliamentary history further, some remarks are necessary to avoid common misunderstandings regarding the whole character of the period that lies before us. Looked at in the democratic way, the period of the Legislative National Assembly is concerned with what the period of the Constituent Assembly was concerned, *viz.*, the simple struggle between republicans and royalists. The movement itself, however, they sum up in the stock word "reaction"—a night in which all cats are grey and which permits them to reel off their night-watchman's commonplaces. And, to be sure, at first sight the Party of Order reveals a maze of different royalist factions, which not only intrigue against each other so that each may elevate its own pretender to the throne and exclude the pretender of the opposing party, but also all unite

THE EIGHTEENTH BRUMAIRE

in common hatred of and common onslaughts on the "republic." In opposition to this royalist conspiracy the Mountain, for its part, appears as the representative of the "republic." The Party of Order appears to be perpetually engaged in a "reaction," which directs itself against press, association and the like, neither more nor less than in Prussia, and which, as in Prussia, is carried out in the form of brutal police intervention by the bureaucracy, the *gendarmerie* and the law courts. The "Mountain," for its part, is again just as continually occupied in warding off these attacks and thus defending the "eternal rights of man," as every so-called people's party has done, more or less, for a century and a half. Looking at the situation and the parties more closely, however, this superficial appearance which veils the *class struggle* and the peculiar physiognomy of this period, disappears.

Legitimists and Orleanists, as we have said, formed the two great sections of the Party of Order. Was that which held these sections fast to their pretenders and kept them apart from one another, nothing but lily and tricolour, house of Bourbon and house of Orleans, different shades of royalty, was it the confession of faith in royalty at all? Under the Bourbons, *large landed property* had governed with its priests and lackeys; under the Orleans, high finance, large-scale industry, wholesale trade, that is, *capital*, governed with its retinue of lawyers, professors and orators. The Legitimate Monarchy was merely the political expression of the hereditary rule of the lords of the soil, as the July Monarchy was only the political expression of the usurping rule of the bourgeois *parvenus*. What kept the two sections apart, therefore, was not any so-called principles, it was their material conditions of existence, two different kinds of property, it was the old antagonism of town and country, the rivalry between capital and landed property. That at the same time old memories, personal enmities, fears and hopes, prejudices and illusions, sympathies and antipathies, convictions, articles of faith and principles bound them to one or the other royal house, who is there that denies this? Upon the different forms of property, upon the social conditions of existence rises an entire superstructure of distinct and characteristically formed sentiments, illusions, modes of thought and views of life. The entire class creates and forms them out of its material foundations and out of the corresponding social relations. The single individual who derives them through tradition and education may imagine that they form the real motives and the starting-point of his activity. If Orleanists and Legitimists, if each section sought to make itself and the other believe that loyalty to their two royal houses separated them, it later proved to be the case that it was rather their divided interests which forbade the uniting of the two royal houses. And as in private life one distinguishes between what a man thinks and says of himself and what he really is and does, still more in historical struggles must one distinguish the phrases and fancies of the parties from their real organism and their real interests, their conception of themselves from their reality. Orleanists and Legitimists found themselves side by side in the republic with equal claims. If each side wished to effect the *restoration* of its *own* royal house against the other, that merely signifies that the *two great interests* into which the *bourgeoisie* is split—landed property and capital—sought each to restore its own supremacy and the subordination of the other. We speak of two interests of the bourgeoisie, for large landed property, despite its feudal coquetry and pride of race, has been rendered thoroughly bourgeois by the development of modern society. Thus the Tories in England long imagined that they were enthusiastic about the monarchy, the church and the beauties of the old English Constitution, until the day of danger wrung from them the confession that they are only enthusiastic about *ground rent*.

The royalists in coalition carried on their intrigues against one another in the press, in Ems, in Claremont,[21] outside Parliament. Behind the scenes they donned their old Orleanist and Legitimist liveries again and engaged in their old tourneys once more. But on the public stage, in their principal and state actions, as a great parliamentary party, they put off their respective royal houses with formal obeisances and adjourn the restoration of the monarchy *in infinitum*.* They do their real business as the *Party*

---

* To infinity.—*Ed.*

THE EIGHTEENTH BRUMAIRE

of Order, that is, under a *social,* not under a *political* title; as representatives of the bourgeois world-order, not as knights of errant princesses; as the bourgeois class against other classes, not as royalists against the republicans. And as the Party of Order they exercised more absolute and sterner domination over the other classes of society than ever previously during the Restoration or during the July Monarchy, a domination which, in general, was only possible under the form of the parliamentary republic, for only under this form could the two great divisions of the French bourgeoisie unite, and therefore put the rule of their class instead of the regime of a privileged section of it on the order of the day. If, nevertheless, they, as the Party of Order, also insult the republic and express their repugnance to it, this happens not merely from royalist memories. Instinct taught them that the republic, indeed, perfects their political rule, but at the same time undermines its social foundation, since they must now confront the subjugated classes and contend against them without intermediation, without the concealment afforded by the crown, without being able to divert the national interest through their subordinate struggles with one another and with the monarchy. It was a feeling of weakness that caused them to recoil from the pure conditions of their own class rule and to sigh for the more incomplete, more undeveloped and consequently less dangerous forms of this rule. On the other hand, as often as the royalists in coalition come in conflict with the pretender that confronts them, with Bonaparte, as often as they believe their parliamentary omnipotence endangered by the executive power, as often, therefore, as they must put forward the political title to their rule, they come forward as *republicans* and not as *royalists,* from the Orleanist Thiers, who warns the National Assembly that the republic divides them least, to the Legitimist Berryer, who, as a tribune swathed in a tricoloured sash, harangues the people assembled before the town hall of the tenth *arrondissement* * on December 2, 1851, in the name of the republic. To be sure, a mocking echo calls back to him: Henry V! Henry V!

* District of a French Department; in Paris, a ward of the city.—*Ed.*

OF LOUIS BONAPARTE

As against the coalition of the bourgeoisie, a coalition between petty bourgeois and workers had been formed, the so-called *Social Democratic* Party. The petty bourgeoisie saw that they were badly rewarded after the June days of 1848, their material interests imperilled and the democratic guarantees which were to ensure the enforcement of these interests endangered by the counter-revolution. Accordingly, they came closer to the workers. On the other hand, their parliamentary representation, the Mountain, thrust aside during the dictatorship of the bourgeois republicans, had in the last half of the life of the Constituent Assembly reconquered its lost popularity through the struggle with Bonaparte and the royalist ministers. It had concluded an alliance with the socialist leaders. In February 1849, banquets celebrated the reconciliation. A joint programme was drafted, joint election committees were set up and joint candidates put forward. From the social demands of the proletariat the revolutionary point was broken off and a democratic turn given to them; from the democratic claims of the petty bourgeoisie the purely political form was stripped off and their socialist point thrust forward. Thus arose *Social Democracy*. The new *Mountain*, the result of this combination, apart from some supernumeraries from the working class and some socialist sectarians, contained the same elements as the old Mountain, only numerically stronger. But in the course of development it had changed with the class that it represented. The peculiar character of Social Democracy is epitomised in the fact that democratic-republican institutions are demanded not as a means of doing away with both the extremes, capital and wage-labour, but of weakening their antagonism and transforming it into harmony. However different the means proposed for the attainment of this end may be, however much it may be trimmed with more or less revolutionary notions, the content remains the same. This content is the transformation of society in a democratic way, but a transformation within the bounds of the petty bourgeoisie. Only, one must not form the narrow-minded notion that the petty bourgeoisie, on principle, wishes to enforce an egoistic class interest. Rather, it believes that the *special* conditions of its emancipation are the *general* conditions under which modern society can alone

THE EIGHTEENTH BRUMAIRE

be saved and the class struggle avoided. Just as little must one imagine that the democratic representatives are all shopkeepers or enthusiastic champions of shopkeepers. According to their education and their individual position they may be separated from them as widely as heaven from earth. What makes them representatives of the petty bourgeoisie is the fact that in their minds they do not go beyond the limits which the latter do not go beyond in life, that they are consequently driven theoretically to the same tasks and solutions to which material interest and social position practically drive the latter. This is in general, the relationship of the *political and literary representatives* of a class to the class that they represent.

After the analysis given, it is obvious that if the Mountain continually contends with the Party of Order for the republic and the so-called rights of man, neither the republic nor the rights of man are its final end, any more than an army which it is desired to deprive of its weapons and which sets about defending itself has taken the field in order to remain in possession of its own weapons.

Immediately on the meeting of the National Assembly, the Party of Order provoked the Mountain. The bourgeoisie now felt the necessity of making an end of the democratic petty bourgeois, as a year before it had apprehended the necessity of settling with the revolutionary proletariat. Only, the situation of the adversary was a different one. The strength of the proletarian party lay in the streets, that of the petty bourgeois in the National Assembly itself. It was therefore a question of decoying them out of the National Assembly into the streets and causing them to smash their parliamentary power themselves, before time and circumstances could consolidate it. The Mountain rushed headlong into the trap.

The bombardment of Rome by the French troops was the bait that was thrown to it. It violated Article V of the Constitution, which forbids the French republic to employ its military forces against the liberties of another people. In addition to this, Article IV also prohibited any declaration of war on the part of the executive power without the assent of the National Assembly, and

OF LOUIS BONAPARTE

by its resolution of May 8, the Constituent Assembly had disapproved of the Roman expedition. On these grounds Ledru-Rollin brought in a bill of impeachment against Bonaparte and his ministers on June 11, 1849. Provoked by the wasp-stings of Thiers, he actually let himself be carried away to the point of threatening that he would defend the Constitution by every means, even by force of arms. The Mountain arose as one man and repeated this call to arms. On June 12, the National Assembly rejected the bill of impeachment, and the Mountain left the parliament. The events of June 13 are known: the proclamation issued by a section of the Mountain, declaring Bonaparte and his ministers "outside the Constitution"; the street processions of the democratic National Guards, who, unarmed as they were, were dispersed in the encounter with the troops of Changarnier, etc., etc. A part of the Mountain fled abroad; another part was arraigned before the High Court at Bourges, and a parliamentary regulation subjected the remainder to the schoolmasterly surveillance of the President of the National Assembly. Paris was again declared in a state of siege and the democratic section of its National Guard dissolved. Thus the influence of the Mountain in parliament and the power of the petty bourgeois in Paris were broken.

Lyons, where June 13 had given the signal for a bloody insurrection of the workers, was, along with five surrounding departments, likewise declared in a state of siege, a condition that has continued up to the present moment.

The bulk of the Mountain had left its advance guard in the lurch, having refused to subscribe to its proclamation. The press had deserted, only two journals having dared to publish the *pronunciamento*. The petty bourgeois betrayed their representatives, in that the National Guards either stayed away or, where they appeared, hindered the erection of barricades. The representatives had duped the petty bourgeois, in that the alleged allies from the army were nowhere to be seen. Finally, instead of gaining an accession of strength from it, the democratic party had infected the proletariat with its own weakness and, as usual with the great deeds of democrats, the leaders had the satisfaction of being able

THE EIGHTEENTH BRUMAIRE

to charge their "people" with desertion, and the people the satisfaction of being able to charge its leaders with selling it.

Seldom had an action been announced with more noise than the impending campaign of the Mountain, seldom had an event been trumpeted with greater certainty or longer in advance than the inevitable victory of democracy. Most assuredly: the democrats believe in the trumpets before whose blasts the walls of Jericho fell down. And as often as they stand before the ramparts of despotism, they seek to imitate the miracle. If the Mountain wished to triumph in parliament, it should not have called to arms. If it called to arms in parliament, it should not have acted in parliamentary fashion on the streets. If the peaceful demonstration was seriously intended, then it was folly not to foresee that it would be given a warlike reception. If a real struggle was intended, then it was a queer idea to lay down the weapons with which it must be waged. But the revolutionary threats of the petty bourgeois and their democratic representatives are mere attempts to intimidate the antagonist. And when they have run into a blind alley, when they have sufficiently compromised themselves to make it necessary to give effect to their threats, then this happens in an ambiguous fashion that avoids nothing so much as the means to the end and tries to find an excuse for defeat. The blaring overture that announced the struggle dies away in a dejected snarl as soon as the struggle has to begin, the actors cease to take themselves *au sérieux*,* and the action collapses completely, like a pricked balloon.

No party exaggerates its powers more than the democrats, none deludes itself more irresponsibly over the situation. When a section of the army had voted for it, the Mountain was now convinced that the army would revolt for it. And on what grounds? On grounds which, from the standpoint of the troops, had no other meaning than that the revolutionaries took the side of the Roman soldiers against the French soldiers. On the other hand, the recollections of June 1848, were still too fresh to allow of anything but a profound aversion on the part of the proletariat towards the National Guard and a thorough-going mistrust of the democratic

* Seriously.—*Ed.*

chiefs on the part of the leaders of the secret societies. To make up for these differences, it was necessary for great, common interests to be at stake. The violation of an abstract paragraph of the Constitution could not provide these interests. Had not the Constitution been repeatedly violated, according to the assurance of the democrats themselves? Had not the most popular journals branded it as counter-revolutionary botch-work? But the democrat, because he represents the petty bourgeoisie, therefore a *transition class*, in which the interests of two classes are simultaneously deadened, imagines himself elevated above class antagonism generally. The democrats concede that a privileged class confronts them, but they, along with all the rest of the surrounding nation, form the *people*. What they represent are the *people's rights;* what interests them are the *people's interests*. Accordingly, when a struggle is impending, they do not need to examine the interests and positions of the different classes. They do not need to consider their own resources too critically. They have merely to give the signal and the people, with all its inexhaustible resources, will fall upon the *oppressors.* If in the performance their interests now prove to be uninteresting and their power to be impotence then either the fault lies with pernicious sophists, who split the *indivisible people* into different hostile camps, or the army was too brutalised and blinded to apprehend the pure aims of democracy as best for itself, or the whole thing has been wrecked by a detail in its execution, or else an unforeseen accident has for this time spoilt the game. In any case, the democrat comes out of the most disgraceful defeat just as immaculate as he went into it innocent, with the newly-won conviction that he is bound to conquer, not that he himself and his party have to give up the old standpoint, but, on the contrary, that conditions have to ripen in his direction.

Accordingly, one must not imagine the Mountain, decimated and broken though it was, and humiliated by the new parliamentary regulation, as being particularly miserable. If June 13 had removed its chiefs, on the other hand it made room for men of lesser calibre, whom this new position flattered. If their powerlessness in parliament could no longer be doubted, they were also entitled now to confine their actions to outbursts of moral indignation

THE EIGHTEENTH BRUMAIRE

and blustering declamation. If the Party of Order affected to see embodied in them, as the last official representatives of the revolution, all the terrors of anarchy, they could in reality be all the more insipid and moderate. They consoled themselves, however, for June 13 with the profound utterance: But if they dare to attack universal suffrage, ah then—then we'll show them what we are made of! *Nous verrons!**

So far as the *Montagnards*** who fled abroad are concerned, it is sufficient to remark here that Ledru-Rollin, because in barely a fortnight he had succeeded in ruining irretrievably the powerful party at whose head he stood, now found himself called upon to form a French government *in partibus;* that in the measure that the level of the revolution sank and the official stalwarts of official France became more dwarflike, his figure in the distance, removed from the scene of action, seemed to grow in stature; that he could figure as the republican pretender for 1852, and that he issued periodical circulars to the Wallachians and other peoples, in which the despots of the Continent are threatened with the deeds of himself and his confederates. Was Proudhon altogether wrong when he cried to these gentlemen: *"Vous n'êtes que des blagueurs"?* ***

On June 13, the Party of Order had not only broken the Mountain, it had effected the *subordination of the Constitution to the majority decisions of the National Assembly.* And so it understood the republic: that the bourgeoisie rules here in parliamentary forms, without, as in the monarchy, any limitations such as the veto of the executive power or the fact that parliament could be dissolved. This was the *parliamentary republic,* as Thiers termed it. But if on June 13 the bourgeoisie secured its omnipotence within the house of parliament, did it not afflict parliament itself with incurable weakness as compared with the executive power and the people by excluding its most popular part? [22] By surrendering numerous deputies without further ado on the demand of the public prosecutor, it abolished its own parliamentary inviolability. The

---

* We shall see.—*Ed.*
** Members of the Mountain.—*Ed.*
*** You are nothing but windbags.—*Ed.*

OF LOUIS BONAPARTE

humiliating regulations [23] to which it subjected the Mountain exalted the President of the Republic in the same measure as it degraded the individual representative of the people. By branding the insurrection for the protection of the constitutional charter as an anarchic act aiming at the overthrow of society, it prohibited in its own case an appeal to insurrection as soon as the executive power should violate the Constitution against it. And by the irony of history, the general who on Bonaparte's instructions bombarded Rome and thus provided the immediate occasion for the constitutional revolt of June 13, that very *Oudinot* was the man offered by the Party of Order imploringly and unavailingly to the people as general on behalf of the Constitution against Bonaparte on December 2, 1851. Another hero of June 13, *Vieyra*, who was lauded from the tribune of the National Assembly for the brutalities that he had committed in the democratic newspaper offices at the head of a troop of National Guards in the pay of the high financiers, this same Vieyra had been initiated into Bonaparte's conspiracy and essentially contributed to depriving the National Assembly in the hour of its death of any protection by the National Guard.

June 13 had still another meaning. The Mountain had wanted to force the impeachment of Bonaparte. Its defeat was therefore a direct victory for Bonaparte, his personal triumph over his democratic enemies. The Party of Order gained the victory; Bonaparte had only to profit by it. He did so. On June 14 a proclamation could be read on the walls of Paris in which the President, reluctantly and against his will, as it were, compelled by the mere force of events, comes forth from his cloistered seclusion and, posing as misunderstood virtue, complains of the calumnies of his opponents and, while he seems to identify his person with the cause of order, rather identifies the cause of order with his person. Moreover, the National Assembly had, it is true, subsequently approved the expedition against Rome, but Bonaparte had taken the initiative in the matter. After having installed the high priest Samuel in the Vatican once more, he could hope to enter the Tuileries as King David. He had won over the priests.

The revolt of June 13, as we have seen, was confined to a peaceful street procession. No war laurels were therefore to be

4 K. Marx, The 18th Brumaire

THE EIGHTEENTH BRUMAIRE

won against it. Nevertheless, at a time as poor as this in heroes and events the Party of Order transformed this bloodless battle into a second Austerlitz.²⁴ Platform and press praised the army as the power of order, in contrast to the popular masses representing the impotence of anarchy, and extolled Changarnier as the "bulwark of society," a deception in which he himself finally came to believe. Surreptitiously, however, the troops that seemed doubtful were transferred from Paris, the regiments whose elections had turned out most democratically were banished from France to Algiers, the turbulent spirits among the troops were relegated to penal detachments and finally the isolation of the press from the barracks and of the barracks from bourgeois society was systematically carried out.

Here we have reached the decisive turning point in the history of the French National Guard. In 1830 it was decisive in the overthrow of the Restoration. Under Louis Philippe every rising miscarried in which the National Guard stood on the side of the troops. When in the February days of 1848 it evinced a passive attitude towards the insurrection and an equivocal one towards Louis Philippe, he gave himself up for lost and actually was lost. Thus the conviction took root that the revolution could not conquer *without* the National Guard, nor the army *against it*. This was the superstition of the army in regard to bourgeois omnipotence. The June days of 1848, when the entire National Guard, with the troops of the line, put down the insurrection, had strengthened the superstition. After Bonaparte's assumption of office, the position of the National Guard was to some extent weakened by the unconstitutional uniting in the person of Changarnier of the command of its forces with the command of the first military division.

Just as here the command of the National Guard appeared as a subsidiary function of the military commander-in-chief, so the National Guard itself appeared as only an appendage of the troops of the line. Finally, on June 13 its power was broken, and not only by its partial dissolution, which from this time on was periodically repeated all over France, until mere fragments of it were left behind. The demonstration of June 13 was, above all, a demonstration of the democratic National Guards. They had not indeed borne their arms, but had worn their uniforms against the army; precisely in this uniform, however, lay the talisman. The army convinced itself that this uniform was a piece of woollen cloth like any other. The spell was broken. In the June days of 1848 bourgeoisie and petty bourgeoisie as the National Guard had been united with the army against the proletariat; on June 13, 1849, the bourgeoisie let the petty-bourgeois National Guard be scattered by the army; on December 2, 1851, the National Guard of the bourgeoisie itself had vanished, and Bonaparte merely registered this fact when he subsequently signed the decree for its dissolution. Thus the bourgeoisie had itself smashed its last weapon against the army, but could not avoid doing so from the moment when the petty bourgeoisie no longer stood behind it as a vassal, but before it as a rebel, as in general it was bound to destroy all its means of defence against absolutism with its own hand, as soon as it had itself become absolute.

Meanwhile, the Party of Order celebrated the reconquest of a power that seemed lost in 1848 only to be found again, freed from its restraints, in 1849, with invective against the republic and the Constitution, with curses on all future, present and past revolutions, including those which its own leaders had made, and with laws by which the press was muzzled, association abolished and the state of siege regulated as an organic institution.[25] The National Assembly then adjourned from the middle of August to the middle of October, after having appointed a permanent commission for the period of its absence. During this recess the Legitimists intrigued with Ems, the Orleanists with Claremont, Bonaparte by princely tours, and the Departmental Councils in deliberations on the revision of the Constitution—incidents which regularly recur in the periodical recesses of the National Assembly and which I only propose to discuss when they become events. Here it may merely be remarked that it was impolitic for the National Assembly to disappear for considerable intervals from the stage and leave only a single, albeit a sorry, figure to be seen at the head of the republic, that of Louis Bonaparte, while to the scandal of the public the Party of Order fell asunder into its royalist component

THE EIGHTEENTH BRUMAIRE

parts and followed its conflicting desires for Restoration. As often as the confused noise of parliament grew silent during these recesses and its body dissolved in the nation, it became unmistakably clear that only one thing was still wanting to complete the true form of this republic, to make the parliamentary recess permanent and replace the republic's *Liberté, Egalité, Fraternité* by the unambiguous words, Infantry, Cavalry, Artillery!

IV

In the middle of October 1849, the National Assembly met once more. On November 1 Bonaparte surprised it with a message in which he announced the dismissal of the Barrot-Falloux ministry and the formation of a new ministry. No one has ever sacked lackeys with less ceremony than Bonaparte his ministers. The kicks that were intended for the National Assembly were given in the meantime to Barrot and Co.

The Barrot ministry, as we have seen, had been composed of Legitimists and Orleanists, a ministry of the Party of Order. Bonaparte had needed it to dissolve the republican Constituent Assembly, to bring about the expedition against Rome and to break the democratic party. Behind this ministry he had seemingly eclipsed himself, surrendered governmental power into the hands of the Party of Order and donned the modest character-mask that the legally responsible editor of a newspaper wore under Louis Philippe, the mask of the *homme de paille*.* He now threw off his mask, that was no longer a light veil behind which he could hide his face, but an iron mask which prevented him from displaying his own features. He had appointed the Barrot ministry so as to force the dissolution of the republican National Assembly in the name of the Party of Order; he dismissed it so as to declare his own name to be independent of the National Assembly of the Party of Order.

Plausible pretexts for this dismissal were not lacking. The Barrot ministry neglected even the forms of politeness that would have let the President of the Republic appear as a power side by

* Man of straw.—*Ed.*

side with the National Assembly. During the recess of the National Assembly Bonaparte published a letter to Edgar Ney in which he seemed to disapprove of the liberal attitude of the Pope, just as in opposition to the Constituent Assembly he had published a letter in which he commended Oudinot for the attack on the Roman republic. When the National Assembly now voted the budget for the Roman expedition, Victor Hugo, ostensibly out of liberalism, brought up this letter for discussion. The Party of Order with scornfully incredulous outcries stifled the idea that Bonaparte's ideas could have any political importance. Not one of the ministers took up the gauntlet for him. On another occasion Barrot, with his well-known hollow rhetoric, let fall from the platform words of indignation concerning the "abominable machinations" that, according to his assertion, went on in the immediate entourage of the President. Finally, while the ministry obtained from the National Assembly a widow's pension for the Duchess of Orleans, it refused to submit any motion to increase the Civil List of the President. And in Bonaparte the imperial pretender was so intimately bound up with the adventurer down on his luck, that the one great idea, that he was called on to restore the Empire, was always supplemented by the other, that it was the mission of the French people to pay his debts.

The Barrot-Falloux ministry was the first and last *parliamentary ministry* that Bonaparte brought into being. Its dismissal forms, accordingly, a decisive turning point. With it the Party of Order lost, never to reconquer it, an indispensable post for the maintenance of the parliamentary regime, the lever of executive power. It is immediately obvious that in a country like France, where the executive power commands an army of officials numbering more than half a million individuals and therefore constantly maintains an immense mass of interests and existences in the most absolute dependence; where the state enmeshes, controls, punishes, superintends and tutors bourgeois society from its most comprehensive manifestations of life down to its most insignificant stirrings, from its most general modes of being to the private existence of individuals; where through the most extraordinary centralisation this parasitic body acquires an ubiquity, an omniscience, a

THE EIGHTEENTH BRUMAIRE

capacity for swifter motion and an elasticity which has an analogy only in the helpless dependence, in the utter shapelessness of the actual body of society—it is obvious that in such a country the National Assembly forfeited all real influence when it lost command of the ministerial posts, if it did not at the same time simplify the administration of the state, reduce the army of officials as far as possible and, finally, let bourgeois society and public opinion create organs of their own independent of the governmental power. But it is with the maintenance of that extensive state machine in its numerous ramifications that the *material interests* of the French bourgeoisie are interwoven in precisely the closest fashion. Here it finds posts for its surplus population and makes up in the form of state salaries for what it cannot pocket in the form of profits, interest, rents and honorariums. On the other hand, its *political interests* compelled it to increase daily the repressive measures and therefore the means and the personnel of the state power, while at the same time it had to wage an uninterrupted war against public opinion and mistrustfully mutilate and cripple society's organs of independent movement, where it did not succeed in amputating them wholly. Thus the French bourgeoisie was compelled by its class position to annihilate, on the one hand, the vital conditions of all parliamentary power, and therefore of its own, likewise, and to render irresistible, on the other hand, the executive power hostile to it.

The new ministry was called the d'Hautpoul ministry. Not in the sense that General d'Hautpoul had received the rank of Prime Minister. Rather, simultaneously with Barrot's dismissal, Bonaparte abolished this dignity, which certainly condemned the President of the Republic to the status of a legal nonentity, of a constitutional monarch, but of a constitutional monarch without a throne or a crown, without a sceptre or a sword, without irresponsibility, without imprescriptible possession of the highest state dignity, and, worst of all, without a Civil List. The d'Hautpoul ministry contained only one man of parliamentary standing, the Jew *Fould,* one of the most notorious of the high financiers. To his lot fell the ministry of finance. Look up the quotations of the Paris bourse and you will find that from November 1849 onwards the

OF LOUIS BONAPARTE

French *Fonds* * rise and fall with the rise and fall of Bonapartist stocks. While Bonaparte had thus found his ally in the *bourse*, at the same time he took possession of the police by appointing Carlier Chief of Police in Paris.

Only in the course of development, however, could the consequences of the change of ministers come to light. To begin with, Bonaparte had only taken a step forward in order to be driven backward all the more obviously. His brusque message was followed by the most servile declaration of submissiveness to the National Assembly. As often as the ministers dared to make a diffident attempt to introduce his personal fads as legislative proposals, they themselves seemed only to carry out, against their will and as obliged by their position, comic instructions of whose fruitlessness they were persuaded in advance. As often as Bonaparte blurted out his intentions behind the ministers' backs and played with his *"idées napoléoniennes,"*** his own ministers disavowed him from the tribune of the National Assembly. His usurpatory longings seemed to make themselves heard only in order that the malicious laughter of his opponents might not be muted. He behaved like a misunderstood genius, whom all the world takes for a simpleton. Never did he enjoy the contempt of all classes in fuller measure than during this period. Never did the bourgeoisie rule more absolutely, never did it display more ostentatiously the insignia of domination.

I have not here to write the history of its legislative activity, which is summarised during this period in two laws: in the law reestablishing the *wine tax*[26] and the *Education Law*[27] abolishing unbelief. If wine drinking was made harder for the French, they were presented all the more plentifully with the water of truer life. If in the law on the wine tax the bourgeoisie declared the old, hateful French tax system to be inviolable, through the Education Law it sought to ensure among the masses the old state of mind that put up with the tax system. One is astonished to see the Orleanists, the liberal bourgeois, these old apostles of Vol-

---

* Consolidated government stocks. —*Ed.*
** Napoleonic ideas. —*Ed.*

THE EIGHTEENTH BRUMAIRE

tairianism and eclectic philosophy, entrust to their hereditary enemies, the Jesuits, the superintendence of the French mind. But if, in regard to the pretenders to the throne, Orleanists and Legitimists could part company, they understood that to secure their united rule necessitated the uniting of the means of repression of two epochs, that the means of subjugation of the July Monarchy had to be supplemented and strengthened by the means of subjugation of the Restoration.

The peasants, disappointed in all their hopes, crushed more than ever by the low level of corn prices on the one hand, and by the growing burden of taxes and mortgage debts on the other, began to bestir themselves in the Departments. They were answered by attacks on the schoolmasters, who were subjected to the clergy, by attacks on the mayors, who were subjected to the prefects, and by a system of espionage, to which all were subjected. In Paris and the large towns reaction has the very physiognomy of its epoch and challenges more than it strikes down. In the countryside it is dull, coarse, petty, tiresome and vexatious, in a word, the *gendarme*. One comprehends how three years of the regime of the *gendarme*, consecrated by the regime of the priest, were bound to demoralise immature masses.

Whatever amount of passion and declamation might be employed by the Party of Order against the minority from the tribune of the National Assembly, its speech remained as monosyllabic as that of the Christians, whose words were to be: Yea, yea; nay, nay! As monosyllabic on the platform as in the press. Flat as a riddle whose answer is known in advance. Whether it was a question of the right of petition or the tax on wine, freedom of the press or free trade, the clubs or the municipal constitution, protection of personal liberty or regulation of the state budget, the watchword constantly recurs, the theme remains always the same, the verdict is ever ready and invariably runs: "*Socialism!*" Even bourgeois liberalism is declared *socialistic*, bourgeois enlightenment socialistic, bourgeois financial reform socialistic. It was socialistic to build a railway, where a canal already existed, and it was socialistic to defend oneself with a stick, when one was attacked with a dagger.

OF LOUIS BONAPARTE

This was not merely a figure of speech, fashion or party tactics. The bourgeoisie had true insight into the fact that all the weapons which it had forged against feudalism turned their points against itself, that all the means of education which it had produced rebelled against its own civilisation, that all the gods which it had created had fallen away from it. It understood that all the so-called bourgeois liberties and organs of progress attacked and menaced its *class rule* at its social foundation and its political summit simultaneously, and had therefore become *"socialistic."* In this menace and this attack it rightly discerned the secret of socialism, whose import and tendency it judges more correctly than so-called socialism knows how to judge itself; the latter can, accordingly, not comprehend why the bourgeoisie callously hardens its heart against it, whether it sentimentally bewails the sufferings of mankind, or in Christian spirit prophesies the millennium and universal brotherly love, or in humanistic style twaddles about mind, education and freedom, or in doctrinaire fashion devises a system for the conciliation and welfare of all classes. What the bourgeoisie did not grasp, however, was the logical conclusion that its *own parliamentary regime,* that its *political rule* in general was now bound to meet with the general verdict of condemnation as being likewise *socialistic.* As long as the rule of the bourgeois class had not been organised completely, as long as it had not acquired its pure political expression, the antagonism of the other classes, likewise, could not appear in its pure form, and where it did appear, could not take the dangerous turn that transforms every struggle against the power of the state into a struggle against capital. If in every stirring of life in society it saw "tranquillity" imperilled, how could it want to maintain at the head of society the *regime of unrest,* its own regime, the *parliamentary regime,* this regime that, according to the expression of one of its orators, lives in struggle and by struggle? The parliamentary regime lives by discussion; how shall it forbid discussion? Every interest, every social institution is here transformed into general ideas, debated as ideas; how shall any interest, any institution sustain itself as above thought and impose itself as an article of faith? The struggle of the orators on the platform evokes

THE EIGHTEENTH BRUMAIRE

the struggle of the scribblers of the press; the debating club in parliament is inevitably supplemented by debating clubs in the salons and the pot-houses; the representatives who constantly appeal to public opinion give public opinion the right to speak its real mind in petitions. The parliamentary regime leaves everything to the decision of majorities; how shall the great majorities outside parliament not want to decide? When you play the fiddle at the top of the state, what else is to be expected but that those down below dance?

By now stigmatising as *"socialistic"* what it had previously extolled as *"liberal,"* the bourgeoisie therefore confesses that its own interest dictates that it should be delivered from the danger of *governing in its own name*; that, in order to restore tranquillity in the land, its bourgeois parliament must, first of all, be given its quietus; that in order to preserve its social power inviolate, its political power must be broken; that the private bourgeois can only continue to exploit the other classes and to enjoy undisturbed property, family, religion and order on condition that their class be condemned along with the other classes to a like political nullity; that in order to save its purse, it must abandon the crown, and the sword that is to safeguard it must at the same time be hung over its own head like the sword of Damocles.

In the domain of general bourgeois interests the National Assembly showed itself so unproductive that, for example, the discussions on the Paris-Avignon railway, which began in the winter of 1850, were still not ripe for conclusion on December 2, 1851. Where it did not repress or react it was stricken with incurable barrenness.

While Bonaparte's ministry partly took the initiative in framing laws in the spirit of the Party of Order, and partly outdid its harshness in their execution and administration, he, on the other hand, by childishly silly proposals sought to win popularity to bring out the contrast between himself and the National Assembly and to hint at a secret reserve that was only temporarily prevented by the conditions from making its hidden treasures available to the French people. Of this character was the proposal to decree a bonus of four *sous* a day to the non-commissioned officers. Of

OF LOUIS BONAPARTE

this character was the proposal of an honour-loan bank[28] for the workers. Money as a gift and money on loan, it was with prospects such as these that he hoped to allure the masses. Donations and loans—the financial science of the *lumpenproletariat*, whether high or low, is restricted to this. Such were the only springs which Bonaparte knew how to set in action. Never has a Pretender speculated more stupidly on the stupidity of the masses.

The National Assembly flared up repeatedly over these unmistakable attempts to gain popularity at its expense, over the growing danger that this adventurer, whom his debts spurred on and no established reputation held back, would venture a desperate coup. The discord between the Party of Order and the President had taken on a threatening character when an unexpected event threw him back repentant into its arms. We mean the *by-elections of March 10, 1850*. These elections were held with the object of filling once more the representatives' seats that after June 13 had been rendered vacant by imprisonment or exile. Paris elected only Social Democratic candidates. It even concentrated most of the votes on an insurgent of June 1848, on Deflotte. Thus did the Parisian petty bourgeoisie, in alliance with the proletariat, revenge itself for its defeat on June 13, 1849. It seemed to have disappeared from the battle-field at the moment of danger only to reappear there on a more propitious occasion with more numerous fighting forces and with a bolder battle-cry. One circumstance seemed to heighten the peril of this election victory. The army voted in Paris for the June insurgent against Lahitte, a minister of Bonaparte's, and in the Departments largely for the *Montagnards*, who here, too, though not indeed so decisively as in Paris, maintained the ascendancy over their adversaries.

Bonaparte saw himself suddenly confronted with revolution once more. As on January 29, 1849, as on June 13, 1849, on March 10, 1850, he disappeared behind the Party of Order. He made obeisance, he pusillanimously begged pardon, he offered to appoint any ministry it pleased at the behest of the parliamentary majority, he even implored the Orleanist and Legitimist party leaders, the Thiers, the Berryers, the Broglies, the Molés, in brief, the so-called burgraves[29] themselves to take the helm of state. The

THE EIGHTEENTH BRUMAIRE

Party of Order did not know how to take advantage of this moment that would never return. Instead of boldly possessing itself of the power offered, it did not even compel Bonaparte to reinstate the ministry dismissed on November 1; it contented itself with humiliating him by its forgiveness and adding *M. Baroche* to the d'Hautpoul ministry. As public prosecutor this Baroche had stormed and raged before the High Court at Bourges, the first time against the revolutionaries of May 15, the second time against the democrats of June 13, both times because of an *attentat* * on the National Assembly. None of Bonaparte's ministers subsequently contributed more to the degradation of the National Assembly, and after December 2, 1851, we meet him once more as the comfortably installed and highly paid vice-president of the Senate. He had spat in the revolutionaries' soup in order that Bonaparte might eat it up.

The Social Democratic Party, for its part, seemed only to try to find pretexts for putting its victory once again in doubt and blunting the point of its victory. Vidal, one of the newly elected representatives of Paris, had been elected simultaneously in Strasbourg. He was induced to decline election for Paris and accept it for Strasbourg. Instead, therefore, of giving its victory at the polls a definite character and thereby compelling the Party of Order at once to contest it in parliament, instead of thus forcing the adversary to fight at the moment of popular enthusiasm and favourable state of feeling in the army, the democratic party wearied Paris during the months of March and April with a new election agitation, let the popular passions aroused wear themselves out in this new provisional election interlude, let the revolutionary energy satiate itself with constitutional successes, dissipate itself in petty intrigues, hollow declamations and sham movements, let the bourgeoisie rally and make their preparations, and, lastly, allowed the meaning of the March elections to find a sentimentally softening commentary in the subsequent April election by the return of Eugene Sue. In a word, it made an April Fool of March 10.

* Attempt, attack.—*Ed.*

OF LOUIS BONAPARTE

The parliamentary majority understood the weakness of its antagonist. Its seventeen burgraves—for Bonaparte had left to it the direction of and responsibility for the attack—worked out a new electoral law, the introduction of which was entrusted to M. Faucher, who solicited this honour for himself. On May 8 he introduced the law by which universal suffrage was abolished, a residence of three years in the locality of the election imposed as a condition on the electors and, finally, the proof of this residence made dependent in the case of the workers on a certificate from their employers.

In the same measure as the democrats had agitated and raged in revolutionary fashion during the constitutional election contest, equally constitutionally did they now, when it was requisite to prove the serious nature of that victory arms in hand, preach order, majestic calm (*calme majestueux*), a legal attitude, that is to say, blind subjection to the will of the counter-revolution, which imposed itself as the law. During the debate the Mountain put the Party of Order to shame by asserting against its revolutionary passionateness the dispassionate standpoint of the philistine who keeps within the law, and by felling it to earth with the fearful reproach that it proceeded in a revolutionary manner. Even the newly elected deputies were at pains to prove by their decorous and discreet action what a misconception it was to decry them as anarchists and construe their election as a victory for revolution. On May 31, the new electoral law went through. The Mountain contented itself with smuggling a protest into the pocket of the President. The electoral law was followed by a new press law, by which the revolutionary newspaper press was entirely suppressed. It had deserved its fate. The *National* and *La Presse*, two bourgeois organs, were left behind after this deluge as the most advanced outposts of the revolution.

We have seen how during March and April the democratic leaders had done everything to embroil the people of Paris in a sham fight, and how after May 8 they did everything to restrain them from a real fight. In addition to this, we must not forget that the year 1850 was one of the most splendid years of industrial and commercial prosperity, and the Paris proletariat was therefore

THE EIGHTEENTH BRUMAIRE

fully employed. But the election law of May 31, 1850, excluded it from any participation in political power. It cut away from it the very ground of the struggle. It threw the workers back into the position of pariahs, just as they had been before the February Revolution. Since in face of such an event they could let themselves be led by the democrats and could forget the revolutionary interests of their class for a momentary ease and comfort, they renounced the honour of being a conquering power, surrendered themselves to their fate, proved that the defeat of June 1848 had made them incapable of fighting for years and that the historical process would first of all have to go forward again *over* their heads. So far as the petty-bourgeois democracy is concerned, which on June 13 had cried: "But if once universal suffrage is attacked, then we'll show them," it now consoled itself with the contention that the counter-revolutionary blow which had struck it was no blow and the law of May 31 no law. On May 2, 1852, every Frenchman would appear at the polling-place with ballot-paper in one hand and sword in the other. With this prophecy it rested content. Finally, just as for the elections of May 29, 1849, so for those of March and April, 1850, the army was punished by its chiefs. This time, however, it said decidedly: "The revolution shall not dupe us a third time."

The law of May 31, 1850, was the *coup d'état* of the bourgeoisie. All its conquests over the revolution hitherto had only a provisional character. They were endangered as soon as the existing National Assembly retired from the stage. They depended on the hazards of a new general election, and the history of elections since 1848 irrefutably proved that in the same measure as the actual domination of the bourgeoisie developed in fact, its moral domination over the mass of the people was lost. On March 10, universal suffrage declared itself directly against the domination of the bourgeoisie; the bourgeoisie answered by outlawing universal suffrage. The law of May 31 was therefore one of the necessities of the class struggle. On the other hand, the Constitution required a minimum of two million votes in order that the election of the President of the Republic might be valid. If none of the candidates for the Presidency received this minimum, the National Assembly was then to choose the President from among the three candidates to whom the largest number of votes would fall. At the time when the Constituent Assembly made this law, ten million electors were registered on the rolls of voters. In its view therefore, a fifth of the people entitled to vote was sufficient to make the presidential election valid. The law of May 31 struck at least three million votes off the electoral rolls, reduced the number of the people entitled to vote to seven millions and, nevertheless, retained the legal minimum of two millions for the presidential election. It therefore raised the legal minimum from a fifth to nearly a third of the effective votes, that is, it did everything to smuggle the election of the President out of the hands of the people and into the hands of the National Assembly. Through the electoral law of May 31 the Party of Order thus seemed to have made its rule doubly secure, since it left the election of the National Assembly and that of the President of the Republic to the stationary section of society.

V

As soon as the revolutionary crisis had been weathered and universal suffrage abolished, the struggle between the National Assembly and Bonaparte immediately broke out again.

The Constitution had fixed Bonaparte's salary at 600,000 francs. Barely six months after his installation he succeeded in increasing this sum to twice as much, for Odilon Barrot wrung from the Constituent National Assembly an extra allowance of 600,000 francs a year for so-called representation monies. After June 13, Bonaparte had caused similar requests to be voiced, this time without getting a response from Barrot. Now, after May 31, he at once availed himself of the favourable moment and caused his ministers to propose a Civil List of three millions in the National Assembly. A long life of adventurous vagabondage had endowed him with the most developed antennae for feeling out the weak moments when he might squeeze money from his bourgeois. He practised regular *chantage*.* The National Assembly had violated the sover-

* Blackmail.—*Ed.*

THE EIGHTEENTH BRUMAIRE

eighty of the people with his assistance and his cognisance. He threatened to denounce its crime to the tribunal of the people unless it loosened its purse-strings and purchased his silence with three million a year. It had robbed three million Frenchmen of their franchise. He demanded, for every Frenchman put out of currency, a franc having currency, precisely three million francs. He, the elect of six millions, claims damages for the votes out of which he has subsequently been cheated. The Commission of the National Assembly refused the importunate one. The Bonapartist press threatened. Could the National Assembly break with the President of the Republic at a moment when in principle it had definitely broken with the mass of the nation? It rejected the annual Civil List, it is true, but it granted, for this once, an extra allowance of two million one hundred and sixty thousand francs. It thus rendered itself guilty of the double weakness of granting the money and of showing at the same time by its vexation that it only granted it unwillingly. We shall see later for what purpose Bonaparte needed the money. After this vexatious aftermath, which followed on the heels of the abolition of universal suffrage and in which Bonaparte exchanged his humble attitude during the crisis of March and April for challenging impudence to the usurpatory parliament, the National Assembly adjourned for three months, from August 11 to November 11. In its place it left behind a Permanent Commission of eighteen members, which contained no Bonapartists, but did contain some moderate republicans. The Permanent Commission of 1849 had included only men of the Party of Order and Bonapartists. But at that time the Party of Order declared itself in permanence against the revolution. This time the parliamentary republic declared itself in permanence against the President. After the law of May 31, this was the only rival that still confronted the Party of Order.

When the National Assembly met once more in November 1850, it seemed that, instead of the petty skirmishes it had hitherto had with the President, a great and ruthless struggle, a life-and-death struggle between the two powers, had become inevitable.

As in 1849, so during this year's parliamentary recess the Party of Order had broken up into its separate sections, each occupied

OF LOUIS BONAPARTE

with its own Restoration intrigues, which obtained fresh nutriment through the death of Louis Philippe. The Legitimist King, Henry V., had even nominated a formal ministry which resided in Paris and in which members of the Permanent Commission held seats.

Bonaparte, in his turn, was therefore entitled to make tours of the French Departments, and according to the disposition of the town that he favoured with his presence, now covertly, now more openly divulge his own restoration plans and canvass votes for himself. On these processions, which the great official *Moniteur* and the little private *Moniteurs* of Bonaparte were naturally bound to celebrate as triumphal processions, he was constantly accompanied by associates of the *Society of December 10*. This society dates from the year 1849. On the pretext of founding a benevolent society, the *lumpenproletariat* of Paris had been organised into secret sections, each section being led by Bonapartist agents, with a Bonapartist general at the head of the whole. Alongside decayed *roués** with doubtful means of subsistence and of doubtful origin, alongside ruined and adventurous offshoots of the bourgeoisie, were vagabonds, discharged soldiers, discharged jail-birds, escaped galley-slaves, swindlers, mountebanks, *lazzaroni*,** pickpockets, tricksters, gamblers, *maquereaux*,*** brothel-keepers, porters, *literati*,**** organ-grinders, rag-pickers, knife-grinders, tinkers, beggars, in short the whole indefinite, disintegrated mass thrown hither and thither, which the French term *la Bohème*; from this kindred element Bonaparte formed the basis of the Society of December 10. A "benevolent society"—in so far as, like Bonaparte, all its members felt the need of benefiting themselves at the expense of the working nation. This Bonaparte, who constitutes himself chief of the *lumpenproletariat*, who here alone rediscovers in mass form the interests which he personally pursues, who recognises in this scum, offal, refuse of all classes, the only class weapon upon which he can base himself unconditionally, he is the real Bonaparte, the Bonaparte *sans phrase*.***** An old crafty

---
* Rakes.—*Ed.*
** The name originally given to the lumpenproletariat of Naples.—*Ed.*
*** Procurers.—*Ed.*
**** Literary agents.—*Ed.*
***** Without circumlocution.—*Ed.*

5 K. Marx, The 18th Brumaire

THE EIGHTEENTH BRUMAIRE

roué, he conceives the historical life of the nations and their principal and state actions as comedy in the most vulgar sense, as a masquerade where the grand costumes, words and postures merely serve to mask the pettiest knavishness. Thus on his expedition to Strasbourg,[30] when a trained Swiss vulture had played the part of the Napoleonic eagle. For his irruption into Boulogne he puts some London lackeys into French uniforms. They represent the army. In his Society of December 10, he assembles ten thousand rascally fellows, who must play the part of the people, as Klaus Zettel that of the lion.* At a moment when the French bourgeoisie itself played the most complete comedy, but in the most serious manner in the world, without infringing any of the pedantic conditions of French dramatic etiquette, and was itself half deceived, half convinced by the solemnity of its own principal and state actions, the adventurer who took the comedy as plain comedy was bound to conquer. Only when he has eliminated his solemn opponent, when he himself now takes his imperial role seriously and with the Napoleonic mask thinks to play the part of the real Napoleon, does he become the victim of his own conception of the world, the serious buffoon, who no longer takes world history for a comedy, but his comedy for world history. What the *National Ateliers*** were for the socialist workers, what the *Gardes Mobiles**** were for the bourgeois republicans, the Society of December 10 was for Bonaparte, the party fighting force peculiar to him. On his journeys the detachments of this society packing the railways had to improvise a public for him, display the public enthusiasm, howl *vive l'Empereur*,**** insult and thrash the republicans, of course under the protection of the police. On his return journeys to Paris they had to form the advance guard, forestall counter-demonstrations or disperse them. The Society of December 10 belonged to him, it was *his* work, his very own idea. What ever else he appropriates, is put into his hands by the forces of circumstance; what-

---

* The reference is to Nick Bottom, the weaver (Klaus Zettel) in Shakespeare's comedy, *A Midsummer Night's Dream.—Ed.*
** Workshops.—*Ed.*
*** Mobile Guards.—*Ed.*
**** Long live the Emperor.—*Ed.*

OF LOUIS BONAPARTE

ever else he does, the circumstances do for him or he is content to copy from the deeds of others. But Bonaparte with the official phrases of order, religion, family, property in public before the citizens, behind him the secret society of the Schufterles and Spiegelbergs,* the society of disorder, prostitution and theft, that is Bonaparte himself as original author, and the history of the Society of December 10 is his own history. Now it had happened by way of exception that popular representatives belonging to the Party of Order came under the cudgels of the Decembrists. Still more. Yon, the police-inspector assigned to the National Assembly and charged with watching over its safety, acting on the information given by a certain Alais, advised the Permanent Commission that a section of the Decembrists had determined to assassinate General Changarnier and Dupin, the President of the National Assembly, and had already fixed the individuals who were to do it. One comprehends the terror of M. Dupin. A parliamentary enquiry into the Society of December 10, that is, the profanation of the Bonapartist secret world, seemed inevitable. Just before the meeting of the National Assembly Bonaparte providently disbanded his society, naturally only on paper, for in a detailed memoir at the end of 1851 Police-Prefect Carlier still sought in vain to move him to a real dispersal of the Decembrists.

The Society of December 10 was thus to remain the private army of Bonaparte until he succeeded in transforming the public army into a Society of December 10. Bonaparte made the first attempt at this shortly after the adjournment of the National Assembly, and indeed with the money just wrested from it. As a fatalist, he lives in the conviction that there are certain higher powers which man, and the soldier in particular, cannot withstand. Among these powers he counts, first and foremost, cigars and champagne, cold poultry and garlic sausage. To begin with, in the apartments of the Elysée he accordingly treats officers and non-comissioned officers to cigars and champagne, to cold poultry and garlic sausage. On October 3 he repeats this manœuvre with the mass of the

---

* Rascally characters in Schiller's drama, *Die Räuber* [The Robbers].—*Ed.*

THE EIGHTEENTH BRUMAIRE

troops at the review at St. Maur and on October 10 the same manœuvre on a still larger scale at the army parade at Satory. The Uncle remembered the campaigns of Alexander in Asia,[31] the Nephew the triumphal marches of Bacchus in the same land. Alexander was a demi-god, to be sure, but Bacchus was a god and, moreover, the tutelary deity of the Society of December 10.

After the review of October 3 the Permanent Commission summoned the War Minister, d'Hautpoul, before it. He promised that these breaches of discipline should not recur. We know how on October 10 Bonaparte kept d'Hautpoul's word. As Commander-in-Chief of the Paris army, Changarnier had commanded at both reviews. He, at once a member of the Permanent Commission, chief of the National Guard, the "saviour" of January 29 and June 13, the "bulwark of society," the candidate of the Party of Order for presidential honours, the suspected Monk* of two monarchies, had hitherto never acknowledged himself as the subordinate of the War Minister, had always openly derided the republican Constitution and had pursued Bonaparte with an ambiguous, lordly protection. Now he was consumed with zeal for discipline against the War Minister and for the Constitution against Bonaparte. While on October 10 a section of the cavalry raised the shout: *"Vive Napoleon! Vivent les saucissons!"*** Changarnier arranged that at least the infantry marching past under the command of his friend Neumeyer should preserve an icy silence. As a punishment, the War Minister relieved General Neumeyer of his post in Paris at Bonaparte's instigation, on the pretext of appointing him commanding general of the fourteenth and fifteenth military divisions. Neumeyer refused this exchange of posts and so had to resign. Changarnier, for his part, published an order of the day on November 2, in which he forbade the troops to indulge in political outcries or demonstrations of any kind while under arms. The Elysée papers*** attacked Changarnier; the papers of the Party of Order attacked Bonaparte; the Permanent Commission held re-

* General Monk who served under Charles I, then under Cromwell and later under Charles II.—*Ed.*
** Long live Napoleon! Long live the sausages!—*Ed.*
*** Bonapartist newspapers.—*Ed.*

peated secret sessions in which it was repeatedly proposed to declare the country in danger; the army seemed divided into two hostile camps, with two hostile general staffs, one in the Elysée, where Bonaparte resided, the other in the Tuileries, the quarters of Changarnier. It seemed that only the meeting of the National Assembly was needed to give the signal for battle. The French public judged this friction between Bonaparte and Changarnier like that English journalist who has characterised it in the following words: "The political housemaids of France are sweeping away the glowing lava of the revolution with old brooms and wrangle with one another while they do their work."

Meanwhile, Bonaparte hastened to remove the War Minister, d'Hautpoul, to pack him off in a hurry to Algiers and to appoint General Schramm War Minister in his place. On November 12, he sent to the National Assembly a message of American prolixity, overloaded with detail, redolent of order, desirous of reconciliation, constitutionally acquiescent, treating of all and sundry, but not of the *questions brûlantes** of the moment. As if in passing, he made the remark that according to the express provisions of the Constitution the President alone disposed over the army. The message closed with the following lofty words:

"Above all things, France demands tranquillity. . . . But bound by an oath, I shall keep within the narrow limits that it has set for me. . . . As far as I am concerned, elected by the people and owing my power to it alone, I shall always bow to its lawfully expressed will. Should you resolve in this session on the revision of the Constitution, a Constituent Assembly will then regulate the position of the executive power. If not, then the people will solemnly pronounce its decision in 1852. But whatever the solutions of the future may be, let us come to an understanding, so that passion, surprise or violence may never decide the destiny of a great nation. . . . What occupies my attention, above all, is not who will rule France in 1852, but how to employ the time which remains at my disposal so that the intervening period may pass by without agitation or disturbance. I have opened my heart to you with sincerity; you will answer my frankness with your trust, my good endeavours with your co-operation, and God will do the rest."

The respectable, hypocritically moderate, virtuously commonplace language of the bourgeoisie reveals its deepest meaning in the mouth of the autocrat of the Society of December 10 and the picnic hero of Saint-Maur and Satory.

* Burning questions.—*Ed.*

THE EIGHTEENTH BRUMAIRE

The burgraves of the Party of Order did not delude themselves for a moment concerning the trust that this opening of the heart deserved. About oaths they had long been blasé, they numbered in their midst veterans and virtuosos of political perjury; they had not failed to hear the passage about the army. They observed with annoyance that in its discursive enumeration of lately enacted laws the message passed over the most important law, the electoral law, in studied silence, and, moreover, in the event of there being no revision of the Constitution, left the election of the President in 1852 in the hands of the people. The electoral law was the leaden ball chained to the feet of the Party of Order, which hindered it in walking and now even prevented it from storming forward! Moreover, by the official disbanding of the Society of December 10 and the dismissal of the War Minister, d'Hautpoul, Bonaparte had with his own hand sacrificed the scapegoats on the altar of the country. He had deprived the expected collision of its sharpness. Finally, the Party of Order itself anxiously sought to avoid, to mitigate, to palliate any decisive conflict with the executive power. From fear of losing their conquests over the revolution, they allowed their rivals to carry off the fruits of these. "Above all things, France demands tranquillity." This was what the Party of Order had cried to the revolution since February, this was what Bonaparte cried to the Party of Order in his message: "Above all things, France demands tranquillity." Bonaparte perpetrated acts that aimed at usurpation, but the Party of Order was guilty of "unrest" if it raised the alarm about these acts and construed them hypochondriacally. The sausages of Satory were quiet as mice when no one spoke of them. "Above all things, France demands tranquillity." Bonaparte demanded, therefore, that he be left in peace to do as he liked and the parliamentary party was paralysed by a double fear, by the fear of again evoking revolutionary unrest and by the fear of itself appearing as the instigator of unrest in the eyes of its own class, in the eyes of the bourgeoisie. Consequently, since France demanded tranquillity above all things, the Party of Order dared not answer "war" after Bonaparte had talked "peace" in his message. The public, which had flattered itself that there would be scenes or great scandal on the

OF LOUIS BONAPARTE

opening of the National Assembly, was cheated of its expectations. The opposition deputies, who demanded the submission of the Permanent Commission's minutes on the October events, were outvoted by the majority. On principle, all debates that might cause excitement were avoided. The activities of the National Assembly during November and December 1850 were without interest.

At last, towards the end of December, guerilla warfare began over individual prerogatives of parliament. The movement got bogged in petty chicaneries regarding the prerogatives of the two powers, since the bourgeoisie had done away with the class struggle for the moment by abolishing universal suffrage.

A judgment for debt had been obtained from the court against Manguin, one of the representatives of the people. In answer to the inquiry of the chief magistrate, the Minister for Justice, Rouher, declared that an order of arrest was to be executed against the debtor without further ado. Manguin, therefore, was thrown into the debtors' gaol. The National Assembly flared up when it learned of the assault. Not only did it order his immediate release, but it even had him fetched forcibly from Clichy the same evening, by its clerk. In order, however, to confirm its faith in the sanctity of private property and with the idea at the back of its mind of opening, in case of need, an asylum for *Montagnards* who had become troublesome, it declared imprisonment of the people's representatives for debt permissible after previously obtaining its consent. It forgot to decree that the President of the Republic might also be locked up for debt. It destroyed the last semblance of immunity that surrounded the members of its own body.

It will be remembered that, acting on the information given by a certain Alais, Police-Inspector Yon had denounced a section of the Decembrists for planning the murder of Dupin and Changarnier. In reference to this, at the very first sitting the *quaestors* made the proposal that parliament should form a police force of its own, paid out of the private budget of the National Assembly and absolutely independent of the police-prefect. The Minister for Home Affairs, Baroche, had protested against this invasion of his domain. A miserable compromise on this matter was concluded, according to which the police-inspector of the Assembly was indeed to be

THE EIGHTEENTH BRUMAIRE

paid out of its private budget and to be appointed and dismissed by its *quaestors*, but after previous agreement with the Minister for Home Affairs. Meanwhile criminal proceedings had been taken by the government against Alais, and here it was easy to represent his information as a hoax and through the mouth of the public prosecutor to cast ridicule upon Dupin, Changarnier, Yon and the whole National Assembly. On December 29 the Minister, Baroche, now writes a letter to Dupin, in which he demands Yon's dismissal. The Bureau of the National Assembly decides to retain Yon in his position, but the National Assembly, alarmed by its violence in the Manguin affair and accustomed, when it has ventured a blow at the executive power, to receive two blows from it in return, does not sanction this decision. It dismissed Yon as a reward for his zeal in service and robs itself of a parliamentary prerogative indispensable against a man who does not decide something in the night in order to carry it out by day, but who decides by day and carries it out in the night.

We have seen how on great and striking occasions during November and December the National Assembly avoided or quashed the struggle with the executive power. Now we see it compelled to take it up on the pettiest occasions. In the Manguin affair it confirms the principle of imprisoning the representatives of the people for debt, but reserves the right to have it applied only to representatives obnoxious to itself and wrangles over this infamous privilege with the Minister for Justice. Instead of availing itself of the alleged murder plot to decree an inquiry into the Society of December 10 and irredeemably unmasking Bonaparte before France and Europe in his true character of chief of the Paris *lumpenproletariat*, it lets the collision be degraded to a point where the only issue between it and the Minister for Home Affairs is one as to which of them has the authority to appoint and dismiss a police-inspector. Thus, during the whole of this period, we see the Party of Order compelled by its equivocal position to dissipate and disintegrate its struggle with the executive power in petty squabbles concerning competency, in chicaneries, legal squabbles, and border-line disputes, and to make the most ridiculous matters of form the substance of its activity. It does not dare to take up

OF LOUIS BONAPARTE

the conflict at the moment when this has significance from the standpoint of principle, when the executive power has really exposed itself and the cause of the National Assembly would be the cause of the nation. By so doing it would give the nation its marching orders, and it fears nothing more than that the nation should be set in motion. On such occasions it accordingly rejects the motions of the Mountain and proceeds to the order of the day. The question at issue in its larger aspects having thus been dropped, the executive power calmly awaits the time when it can again take up the same question on petty and insignificant occasions, when this has, so to speak, only a parliamentary local interest. Then the repressed rage of the Party of Order breaks out, then it tears away the curtain from the *coulisses,* then it denounces the President, then it declares the republic in danger, but then, also, its fervour appears absurd and the occasion for the struggle seems a hypocritical pretext or not at all worth fighting about. The parliamentary storm becomes a storm in a teacup; the fight becomes an intrigue; the collision becomes a scandal. While the revolutionary classes gloat with malicious joy over the humiliation of the National Assembly, for they are just as enthusiastic about the parliamentary prerogatives of this Assembly as the latter is about the public liberties, the bourgeoisie outside parliament does not understand how the bourgeoisie inside parliament can fritter away time over such petty squabbles and imperil tranquillity by such pitiful rivalries with the President. It becomes confused by a strategy that makes peace at the moment when all the world is expecting battles, and attacks at the moment when all the world believes peace has been made.

On December 20, Pascal Duprat put a question to the Minister for Home Affairs concerning the Gold Bars Lottery. This lottery was a "daughter of Elysium." Bonaparte with his faithful followers had brought her into the world and Police-Prefect Carlier had placed her under his official protection, although French law forbids all lotteries with the exception of raffles for charitable purposes. Seven million lottery tickets at a franc apiece, the profits ostensibly to be devoted to shipping Parisian vagabonds to Cali-

THE EIGHTEENTH BRUMAIRE

fornia. On the one hand, golden dreams were to supplant the socialist dreams of the Paris proletariat, the seductive prospect of the first prize the doctrinaire right to work. Naturally, the Paris workers did not recognise in the glitter of the Californian gold bars the inconspicuous francs that were enticed out of their pockets. In the main, however, the matter involved a direct swindle. The vagabonds who wanted to open the Californian gold mines without troubling to leave Paris were Bonaparte himself and his debt-ridden Round Table. The three millions voted by the National Assembly had been squandered; in one way or another the treasury had to be replenished. In vain had Bonaparte opened a national subscription for the foundation of so-called *cités ouvrières** and figured at the head of the list himself with a considerable sum. The hardhearted bourgeois waited mistrustfully for him to pay up his share and since this, naturally, did not ensue, the speculation in socialist castles in the air fell straightway to the ground. The gold bars proved a better draw. Bonaparte and company were not content to pocket part of the excess of the seven millions over the gold bars to be allotted in prizes, they manufactured false lottery-tickets, they issued ten, fifteen and even twenty tickets with the same number, financial operations quite in the spirit of the Society of December 10! Here the National Assembly was confronted not with the fictitious President of the Republic, but with Bonaparte in flesh and blood. Here it could catch him in the act, in conflict not with the Constitution but with the *Code Pénal.*** If on Duprat's interpellation it proceeded to the order of the day, this did not happen merely because Girardin's motion that it should declare itself *satisfait**** reminded the Party of Order of its own systematic corruption. The bourgeois and, above all, the bourgeois inflated to become a statesman, supplements his practical meanness by theoretical extravagance. As a statesman he becomes, like the state power that confronts him, a higher being, that can only be fought in a higher, consecrated fashion.

The Assembly itself having guided him with its own hand across

* Workers' cities.—*Ed.*
** Penal Code.—*Ed.*
*** Satisfied.—*Ed.*

OF LOUIS BONAPARTE

the slippery ground of the military banquets, the reviews, the Society of December 10, and finally, the *Code Pénal*, Bonaparte, who precisely because he was a Bohemian, a princely *lumpenproletarian*, had the advantage over a rascally bourgeois that he could conduct the struggle meanly, now saw that the moment had come when he could pass from an apparent defensive to the offensive. The minor defeats meanwhile sustained by the Minister for Justice, the Minister for War, the Minister for Navy and the Minister for Finance, through which the National Assembly signified its snarling displeasure, troubled him little. He not only prevented the ministers from resigning and thus recognising the sovereignty of parliament over the executive power, he could now consummate what he had begun during the recess of the National Assembly, the separation of the military power from parliament, the *removal of Changarnier*.

An Elysée paper published an order of the day alleged to have been addressed during the month of May to the first military division, and therefore proceeding from Changarnier, in which the officers were recommended, in the event of an insurrection, to give no quarter to the traitors in their own ranks, but to shoot them immediately and refuse the National Assembly the troops, should it requisition them. On January 3, 1851, the Cabinet was interpellated concerning this order of the day. For the investigation of this matter it requests a breathing-space first of three months, then of a week, finally of only twenty-four hours. The Assembly insists on an immediate explanation. Changarnier rises and declares that this order of the day never existed. He adds that he will always hasten to comply with the demands of the National Assembly and that in case of a collision it can count on him. It receives his declaration with indescribable applause and passes a vote of confidence in him. It abdicates, it decrees its own impotence and the omnipotence of the army by placing itself under the private protection of a general; but the general deceives himself when he puts at its command against Bonaparte a power that he only holds in fee from the same Bonaparte and when, in his turn, he expects to be protected by this parliament, by his own protégé in need of protection. But Changarnier believes in the mysterious power with

THE EIGHTEENTH BRUMAIRE

which the bourgeoisie has endowed him since January 29, 1849. He considers himself the third power, existing side by side with both the other state powers. He shares the fate of the rest of this epoch's heroes or rather saints whose greatness consists precisely in the great opinion of them that their party exhibits in its own interests and who shrink to everyday figures as soon as circumstances call on them to perform miracles. Unbelief is, in general, the mortal enemy of these reputed heroes and real saints. Hence their majestically moral indignation at unenthusiastic wits and scoffers.

The same evening, the ministers were summoned to the Elysée; Bonaparte insists on the dismissal of Changarnier; five ministers refuse to sign it; the *Moniteur** announces a ministerial crisis, and the Party of Order threatens to form a parliamentary army under Changarnier's command. The Party of Order had constitutional authority to take this step. It merely had to appoint Changarnier President of the National Assembly and requisition any number of troops it pleased for its protection. It could do so all the more safely as Changarnier still really stood at the head of the army and the Paris National Guard and was only waiting to be requisitioned together with the army. The Bonapartist press did not as yet even dare to question the right of the National Assembly directly to requisition troops, a legal scruple that in the given circumstances did not promise any success. That the army would have obeyed the orders of the National Assembly seems probable when one reflects that Bonaparte had to search all Paris for eight days in order, finally, to find two generals—Baraguay d'Hilliers and Saint-Jean d'Angely—who declared themselves ready to countersign Changarnier's dismissal. That the Party of Order however would have found in its own ranks and in parliament the necessary number of votes for such a resolution seems more than doubtful, when one considers that eight days later two hundred and eighty-six votes detached themselves from the party and that in December 1851, at the last hour for decision, the Mountain still rejected a similar proposal. Nevertheless, the burgraves might, perhaps,

* The official government newspaper.—*Ed.*

still have succeeded in spurring the mass of their party to a heroism that consisted in feeling themselves secure behind a forest of bayonets and accepting the services of an army that had deserted to their camp. Instead of this, on the evening of January 6 the Messrs. Burgraves betook themselves to the Elysée in order to make Bonaparte desist from Changarnier's dismissal by means of statesman-like phrases and considerations of statecraft. Whomever one seeks to persuade one acknowledges as master of the situation. On January 12, Bonaparte, made secure by this step, appoints a new ministry in which the leaders of the old ministry, Fould and Baroche, remain members. Saint-Jean d'Angely becomes War Minister, the *Moniteur* publishes the decree dismissing Changarnier and his command is divided between Baraguay d'Hilliers, who receives the first military division, and Perrot, who receives the National Guard. The bulwark of society has been sacked, and if it does not cause any tiles to fall from the roof, on the other hand the quotations on the *Bourse* rise.

By repulsing the army, which places itself in the person of Changarnier at the disposal of the Party of Order, and so surrendering it irrevocably to the President the Party of Order declares that the bourgeoisie has lost its vocation to rule. Already a parliamentary ministry no longer existed. Having now lost, in addition, the lever of the army and National Guard, what forcible means remained to it with which simultaneously to maintain the usurped authority of parliament over the people and its constitutional authority against the President? None. Only the appeal to impotent principles remained to it now, to principles that it had itself always interpreted merely as general rules, which one prescribes for others in order to be able to move all the more freely oneself. The dismissal of Changarnier and the falling of the military power into Bonaparte's hands closes the first part of the period we are considering, the period of struggle between the Party of Order and the executive power. War between the two powers has now been openly declared, is openly waged, but only after the Party of Order has lost arms and soldiers. Without the ministry, without the people, without public opinion, no longer after its Electoral Law of May 31 the representative of the sovereign nation,

THE EIGHTEENTH BRUMAIRE

sans eyes, *sans* ears, *sans* teeth, *sans* everything, the National Assembly had undergone a gradual transformation into an *old French parliament*,[32] that has to leave action to the government and content itself with growling remonstrances *post festum*.*

The Party of Order receives the new ministry with a storm of indignation. General Bedeau recalls to mind the mildness of the Permanent Commission during the recess and the excess of consideration owing to which it has refrained from the publication of its minutes. The Minister for Home Affairs now himself insists on publication of these minutes which by this time have naturally become as dull as ditch-water, disclose no fresh facts and have not the slightest effect on the blasé public. Upon Remusat's proposal the National Assembly retires into its committees and appoints a "Committee for Extraordinary Measures." Paris departs the less from the rut of its everyday routine, since at this moment trade is prosperous, manufactures are busy, corn prices are low, foodstuffs are overflowing and the savings banks receive fresh deposits daily. The "extraordinary measures" that parliament has announced with so much noise fizzle out on January 18 in a no-confidence vote against the ministry without General Changarnier even being mentioned. The Party of Order had been forced to frame its motion in this way, in order to secure the votes of the republicans, as of all the measures of the ministry Changarnier's dismissal is precisely the only one which the republicans approve of, while the Party of Order is in fact not in a position to censure the other ministerial acts which it had itself dictated.

The no-confidence vote of January 18 was passed by four hundred and fifteen votes to two hundred and eighty-six. Thus, it was only carried by a *coalition* of the extreme Legitimists and Orleanists with the pure republicans and the Mountain. It proved, therefore, that the Party of Order had lost in conflicts with Bonaparte not only the ministry, not only the army, but also its independent parliamentary majority, that a body of representatives had deserted from its camp, out of fanaticism for conciliation, out of fear of the struggle, out of lassitude, out of family regard for the

---

* After the event.—*Ed.*

OF LOUIS BONAPARTE

state salaries of relatives, out of speculation on ministerial posts becoming vacant (Odilon Barrot), out of the shallow egoism which makes the ordinary bourgeois always inclined to sacrifice the general interest of his class for this or that private motive. From the first, the Bonapartist representatives adhered to the Party of Order only in the struggle against the revolution. The leader of the Catholic party, Montalembert, had already at that time thrown his influence into the Bonapartist scale, since he despaired of the parliamentary party's prospects of life. Lastly, the leaders of this party, Thiers and Berryer, the Orleanist and the Legitimist, were compelled openly to proclaim themselves republicans, to confess that their hearts were royalist, but their heads republican, that their parliamentary republic was the sole possible form for the rule of the whole bourgeoisie. Thus, they were compelled, before the eyes of the bourgeois class itself, to stigmatise the Restoration plans, which they continued indefatigably to pursue behind parliament's back, as an intrigue as dangerous as it was brainless.

The no-confidence vote of January 18 hit the ministers and not the President. But it was not the ministry, it was the President who had dismissed Changarnier. Should the Party of Order impeach Bonaparte himself? On account of his restoration desires? The latter merely supplemented their own. On account of his conspiracy in connection with the military reviews and the Society of December 10? They had buried these themes long since under simple orders of the day. On account of the dismissal of the hero of January 29 and June 13, the man who in May 1850 threatened to set fire to all four corners of Paris in the event of a rising? Their allies of the Mountain and Cavaignac did not even allow them to raise the fallen bulwark of society by means of an official attestation of sympathy. They themselves could not deny the President the constitutional authority to dismiss a general. They only raged because he made an unparliamentary use of his constitutional right. Had they not continually made an unconstitutional use of their parliamentary prerogative, and particularly in regard to the abolition of universal suffrage? They were therefore reduced to moving within strictly parliamentary limits. And this involved that peculiar malady which since 1848 has spread all over the

THE EIGHTEENTH BRUMAIRE

Continent, *parliamentary cretinism*, which holds those infected by it fast in an imaginary world and robs them of all sense, all memory, all understanding of the rude external world—it involved this parliamentary cretinism when those who had destroyed all the conditions of parliamentary power with their own hands, and were bound to destroy them in their struggle with the other classes, still took their parliamentary triumphs for victories and believed they hit the President by striking at his ministers. They merely gave him the opportunity to humiliate the National Assembly afresh in the eyes of the nation. On January 20 the *Moniteur* announced that the resignation of the entire ministry had been accepted. On the pretext that no parliamentary party any longer had a majority, as the vote of January 18, this fruit of the coalition between Mountain and royalists, proved, and pending the formation of a new majority, Bonaparte appointed a so-called transition ministry, not one member of which was a member of parliament, all being absolutely unknown and insignificant individuals, a ministry of mere clerks and copyists. The Party of Order could now work to exhaustion playing with these marionettes; the executive power no longer thought it worth while to be seriously represented in the National Assembly. The more his ministers were pure dummies, the more manifestly Bonaparte concentrated the whole executive power in his own person and the more scope he had for exploiting it for his own ends.

In coalition with the Mountain, the Party of Order revenged itself by rejecting the presidential grant of one million eight hundred thousand francs, which the chief of the Society of December 10 had compelled his ministerial clerks to propose. This time a majority of only a hundred and two votes decided the matter; twenty-seven fresh votes had therefore fallen away since January 18; the dissolution of the Party of Order was going forward. At the same time, in order that there might not for a moment be any mistake about the meaning of its coalition with the Mountain, it scorned even to consider a proposal signed by a hundred and eighty-nine members of the Mountain for a general amnesty for political offenders. It sufficed for the Minister for Home Affairs, a certain Vaissé, to declare that the tranquillity was only ap-

OF LOUIS BONAPARTE

parent, in secret great agitation prevailed, in secret ubiquitous societies were being organised, the democratic papers were preparing to come out again, the reports from the departments were unfavourable, the Geneva refugees were directing a conspiracy spreading by way of Lyons over all the south of France. France was on the verge of an industrial and commercial crisis, the manufacturers of Roubaix had reduced working hours, the prisoners of Belle Isle were in revolt—it sufficed for even a mere Vaissé to conjure up the red spectre and the Party of Order rejected without discussion a motion that would certainly have won the National Assembly immense popularity and thrown Bonaparte back into its arms. Instead of letting itself be intimidated by the executive power with the prospect of fresh disturbances, it ought rather to have allowed the class struggle a little elbow-room, so as to keep the executive power dependent on it. But it did not feel equal to the task of playing with fire.

Meanwhile, the so-called transition ministry continued to vegetate until the middle of April. Bonaparte wearied and befooled the National Assembly with continual new ministerial combinations. Now he seemed to want to form a republican ministry with Lamartine and Billault, now a parliamentary one with the inevitable Odilon Barrot, whose name may never be missing when a dupe is necessary, then a Legitimist ministry with Vatimesnil and Benoit d'Azy, and again an Orleanist one with Malleville. While he thus keeps the different sections of the Party of Order in tension against one another and alarms them as a whole with the prospect of a republican ministry and the consequent inevitable restoration of universal suffrage, at the same time he engenders in the bourgeoisie the conviction that his honest efforts to form a parliamentary ministry are frustrated by the irreconcilability of the royalist factions. The bourgeoisie, however, cried out all the louder for a "strong government." It found it all the more unpardonable to leave France "without administration," the more a general commercial crisis seemed now to be approaching and made recruits for socialism in the towns, just as the ruinously low price of corn did in the countryside. Trade became daily slacker, the unemployed hands considerably increased, ten thousand workers, at least,

6 K. Marx, The 18th Brumaire

THE EIGHTEENTH BRUMAIRE

were without bread in Paris, innumerable factories stood idle in Rouen, Mühlhausen, Lyons, Roubaix, Turcoing, St. Etienne, Elbeuf, etc. Under these circumstances, on April 11 Bonaparte could venture to restore the ministry of January 18, Messrs. Rouher, Fould, Baroche, etc., reinforced by M. Léon Faucher, whom the Constituent Assembly during its last days had, with the exception of five votes cast by ministers, unanimously stigmatised with a vote of no-confidence for sending out false telegrams. The National Assembly had therefore gained a victory over the ministry on January 18, it had struggled with Bonaparte for three months, in order that on April 11 Fould and Baroche might admit the puritan Faucher as a third party in their ministerial alliance.

In November 1849, Bonaparte had contented himself with an *unparliamentary* ministry, in January 1851 with an *extra-parliamentary* one, and on April 11 he felt strong enough to form an *anti-parliamentary* ministry, which harmoniously combined in itself the no-confidence votes of both Assemblies, the Constituent and the Legislative, the republican and the royalist. This gradation of ministries was the thermometer with which parliament could measure the decrease of its own vital heat. By the end of April the latter had fallen so low that Persigny, in a personal interview, could urge Changarnier to go over to the camp of the President. Bonaparte, he assures him, regards the influence of the National Assembly as completely destroyed, and the proclamation is already prepared that is to be published after the *coup d'état*, which was kept steadily in view but was by chance again postponed. Changarnier informed the leaders of the Party of Order of the death warrant, but who believes that bug-bites are fatal? And the parliament, stricken, disintegrated and death-tainted as it was, could not prevail on itself to see in its duel with the grotesque chief of the Society of December 10 anything other than a duel with a bug. But Bonaparte answered the Party of Order as Agesilaus did King Agis; "*I seem to you an ant, but I shall one day be a lion.*"

VI

The coalition with the Mountain and the pure republicans, to which the Party of Order saw itself condemned in its unavailing

OF LOUIS BONAPARTE

efforts to maintain possession of the military power and to reconquer supreme control of the executive power, proved incontrovertibly that it had lost its independent *parliamentary majority*. On May 29, the mere power of the calendar, of the hour-hand of the clock gave the sign for its complete disintegration. With May 29, the last year of the life of the National Assembly began. It had now to decide for continuing the Constitution unaltered or for revising it. But revision of the Constitution, that implied not only rule of the bourgeoisie or of petty-bourgeois democracy, democracy or proletarian anarchy, parliamentary republic of Bonaparte, it implied at the same time Orleans or Bourbon! Thus the apple of discord fell in the midst of parliament, whereupon the conflict of interests, which split the Party of Order into hostile sections, was bound to blaze up in the open. The Party of Order was a combination of heterogeneous social substances. The question of revision generated a political temperature at which the product again decomposed into its original constituents.

The interest of the Bonapartists in a revision was simple. For them it was above all a question of abolishing Article 45, which forbade Bonaparte's re-election, and the prolongation of his authority. No less simple appeared the position of the republicans. They unconditionally rejected any revision, they saw in it a universal conspiracy against the republic. Since they commanded *more than a quarter of the votes* in the National Assembly and, according to the Constitution, three quarters of the votes were required for a resolution for revision to be legally valid and for convocation of a revising Assembly, they only needed to count their votes to be sure of victory. And they were sure of victory.

As against these clear positions, the Party of Order found itself caught in inextricable contradictions. If it rejected revision, then it imperilled the *status quo*, since it left Bonaparte only one way out, that of force, and since on May 2, 1852, at the decisive moment, it surrendered France to revolutionary anarchy, with a President who lost his authority, with a parliament which had for a long time not possessed it and with a people that thought to reconquer it. If it voted for constitutional revision, then it knew that it voted in vain and would be bound to fail because of the veto

THE EIGHTEENTH BRUMAIRE

of the republicans. If it unconstitutionally declared a simple majority vote to be binding, then it could only hope to dominate the revolution if it subjected itself unconditionally to the sovereignty of the executive power, then it made Bonaparte master of the Constitution, of the revision and of itself. An only partial revision, which prolonged the authority of the President, paved the way for imperial usurpation. A general revision which shortened the existence of the republic, brought the dynastic claims into unavoidable conflict, for the conditions of a Bourbon and the conditions of an Orleanist Restoration were not only different, they were mutually exclusive.

The *parliamentary republic* was more than the neutral territory on which the two factors of the French bourgeoisie, Legitimists and Orleanists, large landed property and industry, could dwell side by side with equality of rights. It was the unavoidable condition of their *common* rule, the sole form of state in which their general class interest subjected to itself at the same time both the claims of their particular sections and all the remaining classes of society. As royalists they fell back into their antagonism, into the struggle for the supremacy of landed property or of money, and the highest expression of this antagonism, its personification, was their kings themselves, their dynasties. Hence the resistance of the Party of Order to the *recall of the Bourbons.*

The Orleanist and representative of the people, Creton, had in 1849, 1850 and 1851 periodically introduced a motion for the revocation of the decree exiling the royal families. Just as regularly parliament presented the spectacle of an Assembly of royalists that obdurately barred the gates through which their exiled kings might return home. Richard III had murdered Henry VI with the remark that he was too good for this world and belonged in heaven. They declared France too bad to possess her kings again. Constrained by force of circumstances, they had become republicans and repeatedly sanctioned the plebiscite that banished their kings from France.

The revision of the Constitution—and circumstances compelled taking it into consideration—called in question the common rule of the two bourgeois sections along with the republic, and revived, with the possibility of a monarchy, the rivalry of the interests which had alternately predominated in representing it, the struggle for the supremacy of one section over the other. The diplomats of the Party of Order believed they could settle the struggle by a unification of the two dynasties, by a so-called *fusion* of the royalist parties and their royal houses. The real fusion of the Restoration and the July Monarchy was the parliamentary republic, in which Orleanist and Legitimist colours were obliterated and the various species of bourgeois disappeared in the bourgeois as such, in the bourgeois genus. Now, however, Orleanist was to become Legitimist and Legitimist Orleanist. Monarchy, in which their antagonism was personified, was to embody their unity, the expression of their exclusive factional interests to become the expression of their common class interest, the monarchy to do that which only the abolition of two monarchies, the republic, could do and had done. This was the philosopher's stone, to produce which the doctors of the Party of Order racked their brains. As if the Legitimist monarchy could ever become the monarchy of the industrial bourgeois or the bourgeois monarchy ever become the monarchy of the hereditary landed aristocracy. As if landed property and industry could fraternise under one crown, when the crown could only descend to one head, the head of the elder brother or of the younger. As if industry could come to terms with landed property at all, so long as landed property does not decide itself to become industrial. If Henry V should die tomorrow, the Count of Paris would not on that account become the king of the Legitimists unless he ceased to be the king of the Orleanists. The philosophers of fusion, however, who become more vociferous in proportion as the revision question came to the fore, who had provided themselves with an official daily organ in the *Assemblée Nationale* and who are again at work even at this very moment (February 1852), explained the whole difficulty to themselves by the opposition and rivalry of the two dynasties. The attempts to reconcile the Orleans family with Henry V, begun since the death of Louis Philippe,* but, like the dynastic intrigues generally, only played at while the

---

* Louis Philippe died on August 26, 1850, in Claremont (England).—*Ed.*

THE EIGHTEENTH BRUMAIRE

National Assembly was in recess, during the *entr'actes* behind the scenes and having rather the character of sentimental coquetry with the old superstition than of seriously-meant business—these attempts now became principal and state actions and were enacted by the Party of Order on the public stage, instead of amateur theatricals as hitherto. The couriers sped from Paris to Venice, from Venice to Claremont, from Claremont to Paris. The Count of Chambard issues a manifesto in which "with the help of all the members of his family" he announces not his, but the "national" Restoration. The Orleanist, Salvandy, throws himself at the feet of Henry V. The Legitimist chiefs, Berryer, Benoit d'Azy and Saint-Priest, travel to Claremont in order to persuade the Orleans, but in vain. The fusionists perceive too late that the interests of the two bourgeois sections neither lose in exclusiveness nor gain in pliancy when they become accentuated in the form of family interests, interests of two royal houses. If Henry V recognised the Count of Paris as his successor—the sole success that the fusion could achieve at best—the House of Orleans did not in this way win any claim that the childlessness of Henry V had not already secured to it, but it lost all claims that it had conquered through the July Revolution. It waived its original claims, all the titles that it wrested from the Bourbons in almost a hundred years of struggle with the older branch; it bartered away its historical prerogative for the prerogative of its genealogical tree. The fusion was therefore nothing but a voluntary abdication of the House of Orleans, its resignation to Legitimacy, repentant withdrawal from the protestant state-church into the catholic. A withdrawal, moreover, that did not even bring it to the throne which it had lost, but to the throne's steps, on which it had been born. The old Orleanist ministers, Guizot, Duchâtel, etc., who likewise hastened to Claremont to advocate the fusion, in fact represented merely the *Katzenjammer** over the July Revolution, the despair felt in regard to the bourgeois monarchy and the monarchical rule of the bourgeois, the superstitious belief in Legitimacy as the last amulet against anarchy. Imagining themselves mediators between Orleans and Bour-

---
* The "morning-after" feeling.—*Ed.*

bon, in reality they were merely Orleanist deserters, and the Prince of Joinville received them as such. On the other hand, the vital, bellicose section of Orleanists, Thiers, Baze, etc., persuaded Louis Philippe's family all the more easily that if any immediate monarchist restoration presupposed the fusion of the two dynasties, any such fusion, however, presupposed abdication of the House of Orleans; it was, on the contrary, wholly in accord with the tradition of their forefathers to recognise the republic for the moment and wait until events permitted the conversion of the presidential chair into a throne. Rumours of Joinville's candidature were circulated, public curiosity was kept in suspense and, a few months later, in September after the rejection of revision, his candidature was publicly proclaimed.

The attempt at a royalist fusion of Orleanists with Legitimists had thus not only failed, it had destroyed their *parliamentary fusion*, their common republican form, and disintegrated the Party of Order into its original component parts; but the more the estrangement between Claremont and Venice grew, the more their agreement broke down and the more the Joinville agitation gained ground, so much the more eager and earnest became the negotiations between Bonaparte's minister, Faucher, and the Legitimists.

The disintegration of the Party of Order did not stop at its original elements. Each of the two great sections, in its turn, underwent decomposition anew. It was as if all the old nuances that had formerly fought and jostled one another within each of the two circles, whether Orleanist or Legitimist, had thawed again like dry infusoria on contact with water, as if they had acquired anew sufficient vital energy to form groups of their own and independent antagonisms. The Legitimists dreamed that they were back among the controversies between the Tuileries and the Pavillon Marson[33] between Villèle and Polignac. The Orleanists relived the golden days of the tourneys between Guizot, Molé, Broglie, Thiers and Odilon Barrot.

That part of the Party of Order which was eager for revision, but was divided again on the limits to revision, a section composed of the Legitimists led by Berryer and Falloux, on the one hand, and by Larochejaquelin, on the other, and of the conflict-weary

THE EIGHTEENTH BRUMAIRE

Orleanists led by Molé, Broglie, Montalembert and Odilon Barrot, agreed with the Bonapartist representatives on the following indefinite and broadly framed motion: "With the object of restoring to the nation the full exercise of its sovereignty, the undersigned representatives move that the Constitution be revised." At the same time, however, they unanimously declared through their reporter Tocqueville that the National Assembly had not the right to move the *abolition of the republic*, that this right belonged solely to the Revising Chamber. For the rest, the Constitution might only be revised *in a "legal" manner*, hence only if the constitutionally prescribed three-quarters of the number of votes were cast in favour of revision. On June 19, after six days of stormy debate, revision was rejected, as was to be anticipated. Four hundred and forty-six votes were cast for it, but two hundred and seventy-eight against. The extreme Orleanists, Thiers, Changarnier, etc., voted with the republicans and the Mountain.

Thus, the majority of parliament declared against the Constitution, but this Constitution itself declared for the minority and that its vote was binding. But had not the Party of Order subordinated the Constitution to the parliamentary majority on May 31, 1850,* and on June 13, 1849? Up to now, was not its whole policy based on the subordination of the paragraphs of the Constitution to the votes of the parliamentary majority? Had it not left to the democrats the Old Testament superstition in the letter of the law, and scolded the democrats for it? At the present moment, however, revision of the Constitution meant nothing but continuation of the presidential authority, just as continuation of the Constitution meant nothing but Bonaparte's deposition. Parliament had declared for him, but the Constitution declared against parliament. He therefore acted in the sense of parliament, when he tore up the Constitution, and he acted in the sense of the Constitution, when he dispersed parliament.

Parliament had declared the Constitution and, with the latter, its own rule to be "beyond the majority"; by its vote it had suspended the Constitution and prolonged the presidential power, while de-

---

* May 31, 1850—the day the Legislative Assembly revoked universal suffrage.—*Ed.*

claring at the same time that neither the one can die nor the other live so long as it continues to exist itself. Those who were to bury it were standing at the door. While it debated on revision, Bonaparte removed General Baraguay d'Hilliers, who proved irresolute, from the command of the first military division and appointed in his place General Magnan, the victor of Lyons, the hero of the December days, one of his creatures, who under Louis Philippe had already compromised himself more or less in Bonaparte's favour on the occasion of the Boulogne expedition.

The Party of Order proved by its vote on revision that it knew neither how to rule nor how to serve; neither how to live nor how to die; neither how to suffer the republic nor how to overthrow it; neither how to uphold the Constitution nor how to throw it overboard; neither how to co-operate with the President, nor how to break with him. To what, then, did it look for the solution of all the contradictions? To the calendar, to the course of events. It ceased to presume to sway the events. It therefore challenged the events to assume sway over it, and thereby the power to which in the struggle against the people it had surrendered one attribute after another until it itself stood powerless before it. In order that the head of the executive power might be able the more undisturbed to draw up his plan of campaign against it, strengthen his means of attack, select his tools and fortify his positions, it resolved precisely at this critical moment to retire from the stage and adjourn for three months, from August 10 to November 4.

The parliamentary party was not only dissolved into its two great sections, each of these sections was not only split up within itself, but the Party of Order in parliament had fallen out with the Party of Order *outside* parliament. The spokesmen and scribes of the bourgeoisie, its platform and its press, in short, the ideologists of the bourgeoisie and the bourgeoisie itself, the representatives and the represented, faced one another in estrangement and no longer understood one another.

The Legitimists in the provinces, with their limited horizon and their unlimited enthusiasm, accused their parliamentary leaders, Berryer and Falloux, of deserting Henry V and going over to the

THE EIGHTEENTH BRUMAIRE

Bonapartist camp. Their lily minds * believed in the fall of man, but not in diplomacy.

Far more fateful and decisive was the breach of the commercial bourgeoisie with its politicians. It reproached them, not as the Legitimists reproached theirs, with having abandoned their principles, but, on the contrary, with clinging to principles that had become unprofitable.

I have already indicated that since the entry of Fould into the ministry the section of the commercial bourgeoisie which had held the lion's share of power during Louis Philippe's reign, that of the *aristocracy of finance*, had become Bonapartist. Fould represented not only Bonaparte's interests in the *Bourse*, he represented at the same time the interests of the *Bourse* in Bonaparte. The position of the aristocracy of finance is most strikingly depicted by a passage from its European organ, the London *Economist*. In its number of February 1, 1851, its Paris correspondent writes:

"Now we have it stated from numerous quarters that France wishes above all things for repose. The President declares it in his message to the Legislative Assembly; it is echoed from the tribune; it is asserted in the journals; it is announced from the pulpit; *it is demonstrated by the sensitiveness of the public funds at the least prospect of disturbance, and their firmness the instant it is made manifest that the executive is far superior in wisdom and power to the factious ex-officials of all former governments.*"

In its issue of November 29, 1851, *The Economist* declares in its own name: "*the president . . . is the guardian of order, and . . . is now recognised as such on every Stock Exchange of Europe.*"

The aristocracy of finance therefore condemned the parliamentary struggle of the Party of Order with the executive power as a disturbance of order, and celebrated every victory of the President over its ostensible representatives as a *victory of order*. By the aristocracy of finance must here be understood not merely the great loan promoters and speculators in government securities, in regard to whom it is immediately obvious that their interests coincide with the interests of the state power. All modern finance, the whole of banking business, is interwoven in the closest fashion with public credit. A part of their business capital is necessarily invested and put out at interest in quickly convertible government

---

* The lily was the emblem of the Bourbons.—*Ed.*

securities. Their deposits, the capital placed at their disposal and distributed by them among merchants and industrialists, is partly derived from the dividends of holders of government securities. If for the entire money market and the priests of this money market, the stability of the state power has in every epoch signified Moses and the prophets, why not all the more so today, when every deluge threatens to sweep away the old states, and the old state debts with them.

The *industrial bourgeoisie*, too, in its fanaticism for order, was angered by the squabbles of the parliamentary Party of Order with the executive power. After their vote of January 18 on the occasion of Changarnier's dismissal, Thiers, Anglas, St. Beuve, etc., received from their voters in precisely the industrial districts public reproofs in which particularly their coalition with the Mountain was scourged as high treason to order. If we have seen that the boastful taunts, the petty intrigues, which marked the struggle of the Party of Order with the President, merited no better reception, then, on the other hand, this bourgeois party, which required its representatives to allow the military power to go out of the hands of its own parliament into those of an adventurous pretender without offering resistance, was not even worth the intrigues that were squandered on its interests. It proved that the struggle to maintain its *public* interests, its own *class interests*, its *political power*, only troubled and upset it as a disturbance of private business.

With barely an exception, the bourgeois dignitaries of the towns in the departments, the municipal authorities, the judges of the Commercial Court, etc., everywhere received Bonaparte on his tours in the most servile manner, even when, as in Dijon, he made an unrestrained attack on the National Assembly and especially on the Party of Order.

When trade was good, as it still was at the beginning of 1851, the commercial bourgeoisie raged against any parliamentary struggle, lest indeed trade be put out of humour. When trade was bad, as it continually was from the end of February 1851, the commercial bourgeoisie accused the parliamenary struggles of being the cause of stagnation and cried out for them to be ended, 'that trade

THE EIGHTEENTH BRUMAIRE

might become lively again. The revision debates came on just in this bad period. Since the question here was whether the existing form of state was to be or not to be, the bourgeoisie felt itself all the more justified in demanding from its representatives the ending of this torturing provisional arrangement and at the same time the maintainance of the *status quo*. There was no contradiction in this. By the end of the provisional arrangement it understood precisely its continuation, the postponement to a distant future of the moment when it had to reach a decision. The *status quo* could be maintained in only two ways: prolongation of Bonaparte's authority or his constitutional retirement and the election of Cavaignac. A part of the bourgeoisie desired the latter solution and knew no better advice to give its representatives than to keep silent and leave the burning question untouched. They were of the opinion that if their representatives did not speak, Bonaparte would not act. They wanted an ostrich parliament that hid its head in order to remain unseen. Another section of the bourgeoisie, because Bonaparte was already in the presidential chair, desired to leave him sitting in it, so that everything might remain on the old lines. They were indignant because their parliament did not openly infringe the Constitution and abdicate without ceremony.

The General Councils of the departments, those provincial representative bodies of the big bourgeoisie, which met from August 25 onwards during the recess of the National Assembly, declared almost unanimously for revision, therefore against parliament and in favour of Bonaparte.

Still more unequivocally than over the falling out with its *parliamentary representatives* the bourgeoisie displayed its wrath in regard to its literary representatives, its own press. The verdicts of the bourgeois juries, sentencing to ruinous fines and shameless imprisonments for every attack of the bourgeois journalists on Bonaparte's usurpationist desires, for every attempt of the press to defend the political rights of the bourgeoisie against the executive power, astonished not merely France, but all Europe.

If by its clamour for tranquillity the *parliamentary Party of Order*, as I have shown, committed itself to quiescence, if it declared the political rule of the bourgeoisie to be incompatible with the safety and stability of the bourgeoisie, by destroying with its own hands in the struggle against the other classes of society all the conditions for its own regime, the parliamentary regime, then the *extra-parliamentary* mass of the bourgeoisie, on the other hand, by its servility towards the President, by its vilification of parliament, by the brutal maltreatment of its own press, invited Bonaparte to suppress and annihilate its speaking and writing section, its politicans and its *literati*, its platform and its press, in order that it might then be able to pursue its private affairs with full confidence in the protection of a strong and unrestricted government. It declared unequivocally that it longed to get rid of its own political rule in order to get rid of the troubles and dangers of ruling.

And this mass, that had already rebelled against the purely parliamentary and literary struggle for the rule of its own class and betrayed the leaders of this struggle, now dares after the event to indict the proletariat for not having risen in a bloody struggle, a life-and-death struggle on its behalf! This mass, that every moment sacrificed its general class interests, that is, its political interests, to the narrowest and dirtiest private interests, and demanded a similar sacrifice from its representatives, now moans that the proletariat has sacrificed its ideal political interests to its material interests. It poses as a lovely soul that has been misunderstood and deserted in the decisive hour by the proletariat misled by socialists. And it finds a general echo in the bourgeois world. Naturally, I do not speak here of obscure German politicians and riff-raff of this persuasion. I refer, for example, to the same *Economist* that as late as November 29, 1851, consequently four days prior to the *coup d'état*, had declared Bonaparte to be the "guardian of order," but Thiers and Berryer to be "anarchists," and already on December 27, 1851, after Bonaparte had quieted these anarchists, is already vociferous concerning the treason to "the skill, knowledge, discipline, mental influence, intellectual resources and moral weight of the middle and upper ranks" of society committed by "ignorant, untrained, and stupid, *prolétaires*." The stupid, ignorant and vulgar mass was none other than the bourgeois mass itself.

In the year 1851 France, to be sure, had passed through a kind of minor trade crisis. The end of Febuary showed a decline in

THE EIGHTEENTH BRUMAIRE

exports compared with 1850; in March trade suffered and factories closed down; in April the position of the industrial Departments appeared as desperate as after the February days; in May business had still not revived; as late as June 28 the holdings of the Bank of France showed, by the enormous growth of deposits and the equally great decrease in advances on bills of exchange, that production was at a standstill, and it was not until the middle of October that a progressive improvement of business again set in. The French bourgeoisie explained this trade stagnation by purely political causes, by the struggle between parliament and the executive power, by the precariousness of a merely provisional form of state, by the terrifying prospect of May 2, 1852. I will not deny that all these circumstances had a depressing effect on some branches of industry in Paris and the Departments. But in any case this influence of the political conditions was only local and inconsiderable. Does this require further proof than the fact that the improvement of trade set in towards the middle of October, at the very moment when the political situation grew worse, the political horizon darkened and a thunderbolt from Elysium was expected at any moment? For the rest, French bourgeois, whose skill, knowledge, spiritual insight and intellectual resources, reach no further than his nose, could throughout the period of the Industrial Exhibitions in London have found under his nose the cause of his commercial miseries. While in France factories were closed down, in England commercial bankruptcies broke out. While in April and May the industrial panic reached a climax in France, in April and May the commercial panic reached a climax in England. Like the French woollen industry, the English woollen industry suffered, and as French silk manufacture, so did English silk manufacture. If the English cotton factories continued working, this no longer resulted in the same profits as in 1849 and 1850. The only difference was that the crisis in France was industrial, in England commercial; that while in France the factories stood idle, in England they extended operations, but under less favourable conditions than in preceding years; that in France it was exports, in England imports which were hardest hit. The common cause, which is naturally not to be sought within the bounds of the French pol-

OF LOUIS BONAPARTE

itical horizon, was obvious. The years 1849 and 1850 were years of the greatest material prosperity and of an overproduction that appeared as such only in 1851. At the beginning of this year it was given a further special impetus by the prospect of the Industrial Exhibition. In addition there came as special circumstances: first the partial failure of the cotton crop in 1850 and 1851, then the certainty of a bigger cotton crop than had been expected; first the rise, then the sudden fall, in short, the fluctuations in the price of cotton. The supply of raw silk, in France at least, had turned out to be below the average yield. Woollen manufacture, finally, had expanded so much since 1848 that the production of wool could not keep pace with it and the price of raw wool rose out of all proportion to the price of woolen manufactures. Here, then, in the raw material of three industries for the world market, we have already threefold material for a stagnation in trade. Apart from these special circumstances, the apparent crisis of 1851 was nothing more than the halt which overproduction and overspeculation invariably make in describing the industrial cycle, before they gather all their forces in order to rush feverishly through the final phase of this cycle and arrive once more at their starting point, the *general trade crisis*. During such intervals in trade history commercial bankruptcies break out in England, while in France industry itself is reduced to idleness, being partly forced into retreat by the competition of the English in all markets, just then becoming intolerable, and being partly singled out for attack as a luxury industry by every business depression. Thus, besides the general crises, France goes through national trade crises of her own, which are nevertheless determined and conditioned far more by the general state of the world market than by French local influences. It will not be without interest to contrast the judgment of the English bourgeois with the prejudice of the French bourgeois. In its annual trade report for 1851, one of the largest Liverpool houses writes:

"Few years have more thoroughly belied the anticipations formed at their commencement than the one just closed, or shown the fallacy of human calculations more completely, and instead of the great prosperity which was almost unanimously looked for at its opening, it has proved, with the single exception of '47, one of the most discouraging that has been seen for the last quarter of a century—this, of course, refers to the *mercantile*, not to the

THE EIGHTEENTH BRUMAIRE

manufacturing classes. And yet there certainly were grounds for anticipating the reverse at the beginning of the year—stocks of produce were moderate, money was abundant, and has continued so throughout; food was cheap, and no apprehension has ever arisen to the contrary; a plentiful harvest well secured, unbroken peace on the continent, and no political or fiscal disturbances at home; indeed the wings of commerce were never more unfettered. . . . To what source then, is this disastrous result to be attributed? We believe to overtrading both in imports and exports. . . . Unless they [our merchants] will put more stringent limits to their freedom of action, nothing but a *triennial panic* can keep us in check." *

Now picture to yourself the French bourgeois, think how in the throes of this business panic his trade-sick brain is tortured, set in a whirl and stunned by rumours concerning *coups d'état* and the restoration of universal suffrage, by the struggle between parliament and the executive power, by the Fronde war between Orleanists and Legitimists, by the communist conspiracies in the south of France, by alleged *Jacqueries*** in the departments of Nièvre and Cher, by the advertising of the different candidates for the Presidency, by the cheapjack slogans of the journals, by the threats of the republicans to uphold the Constitution and universal suffrage by force of arms, by the gospel-preaching of the *emigré* heroes *in partibus*, who announced that the world would end on May 2, 1852—think of all this and you will comprehend why in this unspeakable, uproarious confusion of fusion, revision, prorogation, Constitution, conspiracy, coalition, emigration, usurpation and revolution the bourgeois madly snorts to this parliamentary republic: "*Rather an end with terror than a terror without end!*"

Bonaparte understood this cry. His powers of comprehension were sharpened by the growing turbulence of creditors who, in each sunset which brought settling day, May 2, 1852, nearer, saw a movement of the stars protesting against their earthly bills of exchange. They had become veritable astrologers. The National Assembly had blighted Bonaparte's hopes of a constitutional prorogation of his authority; the candidature of the Prince of Joinville forbade further vacillation.

---

* Quoted from *The Economist*, Jan. 10, 1852, pp. 29-30.—*Ed.*
** Peasant risings. "Jacques Bonhomme" (John Goodfellow) was the nickname given to the French peasant.—*Ed.*

OF LOUIS BONAPARTE

If ever an event has, well in advance of its coming, cast its shadow before, it was Bonaparte's *coup d'état*. As early as January 29, 1849, barely a month after his election, he had made a proposal about it to Changarnier: In the summer of 1849 his own Prime Minister, Odilon Barrot, had covertly denounced the policy of *coups d'état*; in the winter of 1850 Thiers had openly done so. In May 1851, Persigny had sought once more to win Changarnier for the coup; the *Messager de l'Assemblée* had published an account of their conversation. During every parliamentary storm, the Bonapartist journals threatened a *coup d'état*, and the nearer the crisis drew, the louder grew their tones. In the orgies that Bonaparte kept up every night with men and women of the "swell mob" as soon as the hour of midnight approached and copious potations had loosened tongues and fired imaginations, the *coup d'état* was fixed for the following morning. Swords were drawn, glasses clinked, the representatives were thrown out of the window, the imperial mantle fell upon Bonaparte's shoulders, until the following morning banished the spook once more and astonished Paris learned, from vestals of little reticence and from indiscreet paladins [34] of the danger it had once again escaped. During the months of September and October rumours of a *coup d'état* followed on one another's heels. The shadow took on colour, like a variegated daguerreotype. Look up the events of the month for September and October in the organs of the European daily press and you will find, word for word, intimations like the following: "Paris is full of rumours of a *coup d'état*. The capital is to be filled with troops during the night and the next morning is to bring decrees which dissolve the National Assembly, declare the Department of Seine in a state of siege, restore universal suffrage and appeal to the people. Bonaparte is said to be seeking ministers for the execution of these illegal decrees." The letters that bring these tidings always end with the fateful word *"postponed."* The *coup d'état* was ever the fixed idea of Bonaparte. With this idea he had again set foot on French soil. He was so obsessed by it that he continually betrayed it and blurted it out. He was so weak that, just as continually, he gave it up again. The shadow of the *coup d'état* had be-

7 K. Marx, The 18th Brumaire

THE EIGHTEENTH BRUMAIRE

come so familiar to the Parisians as a spectre, that they were not willing to believe in it when it finally appeared in flesh and blood. It was therefore neither the reticent reserve of the chief of the Society of December 10 nor an unanticipated surprise attack by the National Assembly which allowed the *coup d'état* to succeed. If it succeeded, it succeeded despite his indiscretion and with its foreknowledge, a necessary, inevitable result of the preceding development.

On October 10 Bonaparte announced to his ministers his decision to restore universal suffrage; on the sixteenth they handed in their resignations; on the twenty-sixth Paris learned of the formation of the Thorigny ministry. The Police-Prefect, Carlier, was simultaneously replaced by Maupas; the head of the first military division, Magnan, concentrated the most reliable regiments in the capital. On November 4, the National Assembly resumed its sittings. It had nothing better to do than to recapitulate in a short, succinct form the course it had gone through and to prove that it was only buried after it had died.

The first post that it had forfeited in the struggle with the executive power was the ministry. It had solemnly to admit this loss by accepting the Thorigny ministry, a mere shadow cabinet,[35] as genuine. The Permanent Commission had received M. Giraud with laughter when he presented himself in the name of the new ministers. Such a weak ministry for such strong measures as the restoration of universal suffrage! But the precise object was to accomplish nothing *in* parliament, everything *against* parliament.

On the very first day of its re-opening, the National Assembly received the message from Bonaparte in which he demanded the restoration of universal suffrage and the abolition of the law of May 31, 1850. The same day his ministers introduced a decree in this sense. The National Assembly at once rejected the ministry's motion of urgency and rejected the law itself on November 13 by three hundred and fifty-five votes to three hundred and forty-eight. Thus, it tore up its mandate once more; it once more confirmed the fact that it had transformed itself from the freely elected representatives of the people into the usurpatory parliament of a class; it acknowledged once more that it had itself cut in two the

OF LOUIS BONAPARTE

muscles which connected the parliamentary head with the body of the nation.

If by its motion to restore universal suffrage the executive power appealed from the National Assembly to the people, by its Quaestors' Bill the legislative power appealed from the people to the army. The Quaestors' Bill was to establish its right of immediate requisition of troops, of forming a parliamentary army. If it thus designated the army as the arbitrator between itself and the people, between itself and Bonaparte, if it recognised the army as the decisive state power, on the other hand it had to admit the fact that it had long given up its claim to command this power. By debating its right to requisition troops, instead of requisitioning them at once, it betrayed the doubt about its own powers. By rejecting the Quaestors' Bill, it made public confession of its impotence. This bill was defeated by a hundred and eight votes, the Mountain had thus determined the issue. It found itself in the position of Buridan's ass, not, indeed, between two bundles of hay with the problem of deciding which was the more attractive, but between two showers of blows with the problem of deciding which was the harder. On the one hand, there was the fear of Changarnier; on the other, the fear of Bonaparte. It must be confessed that the position was no heroic one.

On November 18, an amendment was moved to the law introduced by the Party of Order on the municipal elections, to the effect that, instead of three years', one year's domicile should suffice for the municipal electors. The amendment was lost by a single vote, but this one vote immediately proved to be a mistake. Through splitting up into its hostile sections, the Party of Order had long ago lost its independent parliamentary majority. It showed now that there was no majority in parliament at all. The National Assembly had become *incapable of decision.* Its atomic constituents were no longer held together by any force of cohesion; it had drawn its last breath; it was dead.

Finally, a few days before the catastrophe, the extra-parliamentary mass of the bourgeoisie were solemnly to confirm once more their breach with the bourgeoisie in Parliament. Thiers, as a parliamentary hero infected more than the rest with the incurable

THE EIGHTEENTH BRUMAIRE

disease of parliamentary cretinism, had, after the death of parliament, hatched out a new parliamentary intrigue with the Council of State, a responsibility law by which the President was to be firmly held within the limits of the Constitution. Just as, in laying the foundation stone of the new market-halls in Paris on September 15, Bonaparte, like a second Masaniello,[36] had enchanted the *dames des halles*,* the fishwives—to be sure, one fishwife outweighed seventeen burgraves in real power—just as after the introduction of the Quaestors' Bill he enraptured the lieutenants whom he entertained in the Elysée, so now, on November 25, he swept off their feet the industrial bourgeoisie, who had gathered at the circus to receive at his hands prize medals for the London Industrial Exhibition.[37] I give the significant portion of his speech as reported in the *Journal des Débats*:

"With such unhoped for successes, I am justified in reiterating how great the French republic would be if it were permitted to pursue its real interests and reform its institutions, instead of being constantly disturbed by demagogues, on the one hand, and by monarchist hallucinations, on the other. [Loud, stormy and repeated applause from every part of the amphitheatre.] The monarchist hallucinations hinder all progress and all important branches of industry. In place of progress, nothing but struggle. One sees men who were formerly the most zealous supporters of the royal authority and prerogative become partisans of a Convention, merely in order to weaken the authority that has sprung from universal suffrage. [Loud and repeated applause.] We see men who have suffered most from the Revolution and have deplored it most, provoke a new one, and merely in order to fetter the nation's will.... I promise you tranquillity for the future, etc., etc. [Bravo, bravo, stormy bravos.]"

Thus did the industrial bourgeoisie applaud with servile bravos the *coup d'état* of December 2, the annihilation of parliament, the downfall of its own rule, the dictatorship of Bonaparte. The thunder of applause on November 25 had its answer in the thunder of cannon on December 4, and the house of M. Sallandrouze, who had been most lavish with bravos, was the most battered by bombs.

Cromwell, when he dissolved the Long Parliament,[38] went alone into its midst, drew out his watch in order that it should not continue to exist a minute after the period fixed by him, and drove out

* Market women.—*Ed.*

OF LOUIS BONAPARTE

each one of the members of parliament with hilariously humorous taunts. Napoleon, smaller than his prototype, at least betook himself on the Eighteenth Brumaire to the legislative body and read out to it, though in an anxious voice, its sentence of death. The second Bonaparte, who, moreover, found himself in possession of an executive power very different from that of Cromwell or Napoleon, sought his model, not in the annals of world history, but in the annals of the Society of December 10, in the annals of criminal jurisdiction. He robs the Bank of France of twenty-five million francs, buys General Magnon with a million, the soldiers with fifteen francs apiece and liquor, comes together with his accomplices secretly like a thief in the night, has the houses of the most dangerous parliamentary leaders broken into and Cavaignac, Lamoricière, Leflô, Changarnier, Charras, Thiers, Baze, etc., dragged from their beds, the chief squares of Paris and the parliamentary buildings occupied by troops, and cheapjack placards posted early in the morning on all the walls, proclaiming the dissolution of the National Assembly and the Council of State, the restoration of universal suffrage and the placing of the Seine Department in a state of siege. In like manner, he inserted a little later in the *Moniteur* a false document, according to which influential parliamentarians had grouped themselves round him as state advisers.

The rump parliament, assembled in the mayoral building of the tenth *arrondissement* * and consisting mainly of Legitimists and Orleanists, votes the deposition of Bonaparte amid repeated cries of "Long live the republic," unavailingly harangues the gaping crowds before the building and is finally led off in the charge of African sharpshooters, first of all to the d'Orsay barracks, and later packed into prison vans and transported to the prisons of Mazas, Ham and Vincennes. Thus ended the Party of Order, the Legislative Assembly and the February Revolution. Before hastening to a close, let us briefly summarise its history:

I. *First Period.* From February 24 to May 4, 1848. February period. Prologue. Universal brotherhood swindle.

* Ward.—*Ed.*

THE EIGHTEENTH BRUMAIRE

II. *Second Period.* Period of constituting the republic and of the Constituent National Assembly.

1. May 4 to June 25, 1848. Struggle of all classes against the proletariat. Defeat of the proletariat in the June days.

2. June 25 to December 10, 1848. Dictatorship of the pure bourgeois-republicans. Drafting of the Constitution. Proclamation of the state of seige in Paris. The bourgeois dictatorship set aside on December 10 by the election of Bonaparte as President.

3. December 20, 1848, to May 29, 1849. Struggle of the Constituent Assembly with Bonaparte and with the Party of Order in alliance with him. Passing of the Contituent Assembly. Downfall of the republican bourgeoisie.

III. *Third Period.* Period of the *constitutional republic* and of the *Legislative National Assembly.*

1. May 29, 1849, to June 13, 1849. Struggle of the petty bourgeoisie with the bourgeoisie and with Bonaparte. Defeat of the petty bourgeois democracy.

2. June 13, 1849, to May 31, 1850. Parliamentary dictatorship of the Party of Order. It completes its rule by abolishing universal suffrage, but loses the parliamentary ministry.

3. May 31, 1850, to December 2, 1851. Struggle between the parliamentary bourgeoisie and Bonaparte.

(a) May 31, 1850, to January 12, 1851. Parliament loses the supreme command of the army.

(b) January 12 to April 11, 1851. It is worsted in the attempts to regain the administrative power. The Party of Order loses its independent parliamentary majority. Its coalition with the republicans and the Mountain.

(c) April 11, 1851, to October 9, 1851. Attempts at revision, fusion, prorogation. The Party of Order decomposes into its separate constituents. The breach widens between the bourgeois mass and the bourgeois parliament and press.

(d) October 9 to December 2, 1851. Open breach between parliament and the executive power. Parliament performs its dying act and succumbs, left in the lurch by its own class, by the army and by all the remaining classes. Passing of the par-

OF LOUIS BONAPARTE

liamentary regime and of bourgeois rule. Victory of Bonaparte. Parody of imperial Restoration.

VII

On the threshold of the February Revolution, the *social republic* appeared as a phrase, as a prophecy. In the June days of 1848, it was drowned in the blood of the *Paris proletariat,* but it haunts the subsequent acts of the drama like a ghost. The *democratic republic* makes its appearance. On June 13, 1849, it is dissipated together with its *petty bourgeois,* who take to their heels, but in its flight it blows its own trumpet with redoubled boastfulness. The *parliamentary republic,* together with the bourgeoisie, takes possession of the entire stage; it lives out its existence to the full, but December 2, 1851, buries it to the accompaniment of the cry of terror of the royalists in coalition: "Long live the republic!"

The French bourgeoisie offered resistance to the domination of the working proletariat; it has brought the *lumpenproletariat* to domination, with the chief of the Society of December 10 at the head. The bourgeoisie kept France in breathless fear of the future terrors of red anarchy; Bonaparte discounted this future for it when, on December 4, he had the eminent bourgeois of the Boulevard Montmartre and the Boulevard des Italiens shot down at their windows by the army of order, whose enthusiasm was inspired by liquor. It apotheosised the sword; the sword rules it. It destroyed the revolutionary press; its own press has been destroyed. It placed public meetings under police supervision; its salons are under the supervision of the police. It disbanded the democratic National Guard; its own National Guard has been disbanded. It imposed the state of siege; the state of siege has been imposed on it. It supplanted the juries by military commissions; its juries are supplanted by military commissions; it subjected public education to the priests; the priests subject it to their own education. It transported people without trial; it is transported without trial. It suppressed every stirring in society by means of the state power; every stirring in its society is repressed by means of the state power. Out of enthusiasm for its purse, it rebelled against its own politicians and men of letters; its politicians and men of

THE EIGHTEENTH BRUMAIRE

letters are swept aside, but its purse is plundered now that its mouth has been gagged and its pen broken. The bourgeoisie never wearied of crying out to the revolution what Saint Arsenius cried out to the Christians: *"Fuge, tace, quiesce!"* Flee, be silent, keep quiet! Bonaparte cries to the bourgeoisie: *"Fuge, tace, quiesce!"* Flee, be silent, keep quiet!

The French bourgeoisie had long since found the solution to Napoleon's dilemma: *"Dans cinquante ans l'Europe sera républicaine ou cosaque."** It had found the solution to it in the *"république cosaque."*** No Circe, by means of civil magic, has distorted that work of art, the bourgeois republic, into a monstrous shape. That republic has lost nothing but the semblance of respectability. The present-day France was contained in a finished state within the parliamentary republic. It only required a bayonet thrust for the bubble to burst and the monster to spring forth before our eyes.

[The immediate aim of the February Revolution was to overthrow the Orleans dynasty and the section of the bourgeoisie that ruled during its reign. This aim was only attained on December 2, 1851. The immense possessions of the house of Orleans, the real basis of its influence, were now confiscated and what had been expected after the February Revolution came to pass after the December coup—prison, fight, dismissal, banishment, disarming, derision for the men who since 1830 had wearied France with their renown. But, under Louis Philippe only a part of the commercial bourgeoisie ruled. Its other sections formed a dynastic and a republican opposition or were altogether disfranchised. Only the parliamentary republic accepted all sections of the commercial bourgeoisie into its sphere of state. Under Louis Philippe, moreover, the commercial bourgeoisie excluded the landowning bourgeoisie. Only the parliamentary republic set them side by side with equal rights, married the July monarchy to the Legitimist monarchy and fused two epochs of property rule into one. Under Louis Philippe, the favoured section of the bourgeoisie concealed its rule under cover of the crown; in the parliamentary republic the

---

* "Within fifty years Europe will be republican or Cossack."—*Ed.*
** Cossack republic.—*Ed.*

OF LOUIS BONAPARTE

rule of the bourgeoisie, after it had united all its elements and extended its realm to be the realm of its class, revealed its uncovered head. Thus the revolution itself had first to create the form in which the rule of the bourgeoisie could obtain its broadest, most general and final expression, and therefore could now be overthrown without being able to arise again.

Only now was the judgment, passed in February, executed on the Orleanist bourgeoisie, that is, on the most vital section of the French bourgeoisie. Now it was defeated in its parliament, its bar, its commercial courts, its provincial representative bodies, its notaries, its university, its tribune and its tribunals, its press and its literature, its administrative revenues and its court fees, its army pay and its state incomes, in its mind and in its body. *Blanqui* had made the disbandment of the bourgeois guards the first demand on the revolution, and the bourgeois guards, who in February offered the revolution their hand in order to hinder its progress, vanished from the scene in December. The Pantheon itself becomes transformed into an ordinary church. With the final form of the bourgeois regime the spell is likewise broken which transfigured its initiators of the eighteenth century into saints.]

Why did not the Paris proletariat rise in revolt after December?

The overthrow of the bourgeoisie had as yet only been decreed; the decree had not been carried out. Any serious insurrection of the proletariat would at once have put fresh life into the bourgeoisie, would have reconciled it with the army and would have ensured a second June defeat for the workers.

On December 4 the proletariat was incited to fight by the bourgeois and the small shopkeepers. On the evening of that day several legions of the National Guard promised to appear, armed and uniformed, on the scene of action. For the bourgeois and the small shopkeepers had found out that in one of his decrees of December 2, Bonaparte abolished the secret ballot and enjoined them to record their "yes" or "no" in the official registers after their names. The resistance of December 4 intimidated Bonaparte. During the night he caused placards to be posted on all the street corners of Paris, announcing the restoration of the secret ballot. The bourgeois and the small shopkeepers believed that they had

THE EIGHTEENTH BRUMAIRE

gained their end. Those who failed to appear next morning were the bourgeois and the small shopkeepers.

By a *coup de main* during the night of December 1 to 2, Bonaparte had robbed the Paris proletariat of its leaders, the barricade commanders. An army without officers, made disinclined to fight under the banner of the *Montagnards* by the memories of June 1848 and 1849 and May 1850, it left to its vanguard, the secret societies, the task of saving the insurrectionary honour of Paris, which the bourgeoisie had so spinelessly surrendered to the soldiers that, later on, Bonaparte could sneeringly give as his motive for disarming the National Guard—his fear that its arms would be turned against itself by the anarchists!

"C'est le triomphe complet et définitif du socialisme!"*

Thus Guizot characterised December 2. But if the overthrow of the parliamentary republic contains within itself the germ of the triumph of the proletarian revolution, its immediate and obvious result was *the victory of Bonaparte over parliament, of the executive power over the legislative power, of force without phrases over the force of phrases.* In parliament the nation made its general will the law, that is, it made the law of the ruling class its general will. Before the executive power it renounces all will of its own and surrenders itself to the superior orders of something alien, of authority. The executive power, in contrast to the legislative power, expresses the heteronomy** of the nation, in contrast to its autonomy. France, therefore, seems to have escaped the despotism of a class only to fall back beneath the despotism of an individual and, what is more, beneath the authority of an individual without authority. The struggle seems to be settled in such a way that all classes, equally impotent and equally mute, fall on their knees before the club.

But the revolution is thoroughgoing. It is still in process of passing through purgatory. It does its work methodically. By December 2, 1851, it had completed one half of its preparatory work; it is now completing the other half. First it perfected the

---

* "This is the complete and final triumph of socialism."—*Ed.*
** *i.e.*, its dependence on foreign authority.—*Ed.*

OF LOUIS BONAPARTE

parliamentary power, in order to be able to overthrow it. Now that it has attained this, it perfects the *executive power*, reduces it to its purest expression, isolates it, sets it up against itself as the sole target, in order to concentrate all its forces of destruction against it. And when it has done this second half of its preliminary work, Europe will leap from her seat and exultantly exclaim: Well grubbed, old mole!*

This executive power with its enormous bureaucratic and military organisation, with its artificial state machinery embracing wide strata, with a host of officials numbering half a million, besides an army of another half million, this appalling parasitic growth, which enmeshes the body of French society like a net and chokes all its pores, sprang up in the days of the absolute monarchy, with the decay of the feudal system, which it helped to hasten. The seigniorial privileges of the landowners and towns became transformed into so many attributes of the state power, the feudal dignitaries into paid officials and the motley pattern of conflicting mediaeval plenary powers into the regulated plan of a state authority, whose work is divided and centralised as in a factory. The first French Revolution, with its task of breaking all local, territorial, urban and provincial independent powers in order to create the bourgeois unity of the nation, was bound to develop what the absolute monarchy had begun—centralisation, but at the same time the extent, the attributes and the agents of governmental authority. Napoleon perfected this state machinery. The Legitimist monarchy and the July monarchy added nothing but a greater division of labour, growing in the same measure that the division of labour within bourgeois society created new groups of interests, and, therefore, new material for state administration. Every *common* interest was straightway severed from society, counterposed to it as a higher, *general* interest, snatched from the self-activity of society's members and made an object of governmental activity from the bridge, the school-house and the communal property of a village community to the railways, the national

---

* A reference to Shakespeare's *Hamlet*. The actual words are: "Old mole! Canst work i' the earth so fast? A worthy pioneer!"—*Ed.*

THE EIGHTEENTH BRUMAIRE

wealth and the national university of France. The parliamentary republic, finally, in its struggle against the revolution, found itself compelled to strengthen, along with the repressive measures, the resources and centralisation of governmental power. All the revolutions perfected this machine instead of smashing it up. The parties that contended in turn for domination regarded the possession of this huge state edifice as the principal spoils of the victor.[39]

But under the absolute monarchy, during the first Revolution, and under Napoleon, bureaucracy was only the means of preparing the class rule of the bourgeoisie. Under the Restoration, under Louis Philippe and under the parliamentary republic, it was the instrument of the ruling class, however much it strove for power of its own.

Only under the second Bonaparte does the state seem to have made itself completely independent. As against bourgeois society, the state machine has consolidated its position so thoroughly that the chief of the Society of December 10 suffices for its head, an adventurer blown in from abroad, elevated on the shield by a drunken soldiery, which he has bought with liquor and sausages, and which he must continually ply with sausage anew. Hence the downcast despair, the feeling of most dreadful humiliation and degradation that oppresses the breast of France and makes her catch her breath. She feels herself dishonoured.

And yet the state power is not suspended in mid-air. Bonaparte represents a class, and the most numerous class of French society at that, the *small peasants.*

Just as the Bourbons were the dynasty of large landed property and just as the Orleans were the dynasty of money, so the Bonapartes are the dynasty of the peasants, that is, the mass of the French people. Not the Bonaparte who submitted to the bourgeois parliament, but the Bonaparte who dispersed it, is the chosen of the peasantry. For three years the towns had succeeded in falsifying the meaning of the election of December 10 and in cheating the peasants out of the restoration of the Empire. The election of December 10, 1848, was consummated only by the *coup d'état* of December 2, 1851.

OF LOUIS BONAPARTE

The small peasants form a vast mass, the members of which live in similar conditions, but without entering into manifold relations with one another. Their mode of production isolates them from one another, instead of bringing them into mutual intercourse. The isolation is increased by France's bad means of communication and by the poverty of the peasants. Their field of production the small holding, admits of no division of labour in its cultivation, no application of science and, therefore, no multiplicity of development, no diversity of talents, no wealth of social relationships. Each individual peasant family is almost self-sufficient; it itself directly produces the major part of its consumption and thus acquires its means of life more through exchange with nature than in intercourse with society. The small holding, the peasant and his family; alongside them another small holding, another peasant and another family. A few score of these make up a village, and a few score of villages make up a Department. In this way, the great mass of the French nation is formed by simple addition of homologous magnitudes, much as potatoes in a sack form a sackful of potatoes. In so far as millions of families live under economic conditions of existence that divide their mode of life, their interests and their culture from those of the other classes, and put them in hostile contrast to the latter, they form a class. In so far as there is merely a local interconnection among these small peasants, and the identity of their interests begets no unity, no national union and no political organisation, they do not form a class. They are consequently incapable of enforcing their class interest in their own name, whether through a parliament or through a convention. They cannot represent themselves, they must be represented. Their representative must at the same time appear as their master, as an authority over them, as an unlimited governmental power, that protects them against the other classes and sends them the rain and the sunshine from above. The political influence of the small peasants, therefore finds its final expression in the executive power subordinating society to itself.

Historical tradition gave rise to the faith of the French peasants in the miracle that a man named Napoleon would bring all the

THE EIGHTEENTH BRUMAIRE

glory back to them. And an individual was found who gives himself out as the man because he bears the name of Napoleon, in consequence of the *Code Napoléon*,* which lays down that *la recherche de la paternité est interdite*.** After being a vagabond for twenty years and after a series of grotesque adventures, the legend finds fulfilment and the man becomes Emperor of the French. The fixed idea of the nephew was realised, because it coincided with the fixed idea of the most numerous class of the French people.

But, it may be objected, what about the peasant risings in half of France, the hounding of masses of peasants by the army, the mass incarceration and transportation of the peasants?

Since Louis XIV, France has experienced no similar persecution of the peasants "on account of demagogic intrigues."

But let there be no misunderstanding. The Bonaparte dynasty represents not the revolutionary, but the conservative peasant; not the peasant that strikes out beyond the condition of his social existence, the small holding, but rather the peasant who wants to consolidate it; not the country folk who want to overthrow the old order through their own energies linked up with the towns, but on the contrary those who, in stupefied bondage to this old order, want to see themselves with their small holding saved and favoured by the ghost of the Empire. It represents not the enlightenment, but the superstition of the peasant; not his judgment, but his prejudice; not his future, but his past; not his modern Cevennes, but his modern Vendée.[40]

The three years' rigorous rule of the parliamentary republic had freed a part of the French peasants from the Napoleonic illusion and had revolutionised them, even if only superficially, but the bourgeoisie violently repressed them, as often as they set themselves in motion. Under the parliamentary republic the modern and the traditional consciousness of the French peasant contended for mastery. The contest proceeded in the form of an incessant struggle between the schoolmasters and the priests. The bourgeoi-

---

* The French code of civil law, promulgated on March 31, 1804.—*Ed.*
** Inquiry into fatherhood is forbidden.—*Ed.*

OF LOUIS BONAPARTE

sie struck down the schoolmasters. For the first time, the peasants made efforts to behave independently in the face of governmental activity. This was shown in the continual conflict between the mayors and the prefects. The bourgeoisie deposed the mayors. Finally, during the period of the parliamentary republic, the peasans of different localities rose against their own offspring, the army. The bourgeoisie punished them with states of siege and distraints on their goods. And this same bourgeoisie now cries out about the stupidity of the masses, the vile multitude, that has betrayed it to Bonaparte. It has itself forcibly strengthened the imperialism* of the peasant class, it held fast to the conditions that form the birthplace of this peasant religion. The bourgeoisie, to be sure, is bound to fear the stupidity of the masses, as long as they remain conservative, and the insight of the masses, as soon as they become revolutionary.

In the risings after the *coup d'état,* a part of the French peasants protested, arms in hand, against their own vote of December 10, 1848. The school they had gone through since 1848 had sharpened their wits. But they had made themselves over to the underworld of history; history held them to their word, and the majority was still so bound that in precisely the reddest Departments the peasant population voted openly for Bonaparte.** In its view, the National Assembly had hindered his progress. He had now merely broken the fetters that the town had imposed on the will of the countryside. In some parts the peasants even entertained the grotesque notion of a Convention [41] side by side with a Napoleon.

After the first Revolution had transformed the peasants from semi-villeins into freeholders, Napoleon confirmed and regulated the conditions on which they could exploit undisturbed the soil of France which had only just come into their possession and slake their youthful passion for property. But what is now causing the ruin of the French peasant is his dwarf holding itself, the division of the land, the form of property which Napoleon consolidated in France. It is precisely the material conditions which made the

---

* In the sense of imperial sentiments.—*Ed.*

** In the plebiscite that ratified the *coup d'état,* by voting Bonaparte back as President with a huge majority.—*Ed.*

THE EIGHTEENTH BRUMAIRE

feudal peasant into a small peasant and Napoleon into an emperor. Two generations have sufficed to produce the inevitable result: progressive deterioration of agriculture, progressive indebtedness of the agriculturist. The "Napoleonic" form of property, which at the beginning of the nineteenth century was the condition for the liberation and enrichment of the French country folk, has developed in the course of this century as the law of their enslavement and pauperisation. And it is just this law which is the first of the *"idées napoléoniennes"** which the second Bonaparte has to uphold. If he still shares with the peasants the illusion that the cause of their ruin is to be sought not in this small holding property itself but outside it in the influence of secondary causes, then his experiments will burst like soap bubbles when they come into contact with the relations of production.

The economic development of this small holding property has turned the relation of the peasants to the remaining classes of society completely upside down. Under Napoleon, the fragmentation of the land in the country side supplemented free competition and the beginning of big industry in the towns. [Even the favouring of the peasant class was in the interest of the new bourgeois order. This newly-created class was the many-sided extension of the bourgeois regime beyond the gates of the towns, its realisation on a national scale.] This class was the ubiquitous protest against the landed aristocracy which had just been overthrown.

[If it was favoured above all, it, above all, offered the point of attack for the restoration of the feudal lands.]

The roots that this small holding property struck in French soil deprived feudalism of all nutriment. Its landmarks formed the natural fortifications of the bourgeoisie against any *coup de main* on the part of its old overlords. But in the course of the nineteenth century the feudal lords were replaced by urban usurers; the feudal obligation that went with the land was replaced by the mortgage; aristocratic landed property was replaced by bourgeois capital. The small holding of the peasant is now only the pretext that allows the capitalist to draw profits, interest and rent from the

---

* Napoleonic ideas.

OF LOUIS BONAPARTE

soil, while leaving it to the tiller of the soil himself to see how he can extract his wages. The mortgage debt burdening the soil of France imposes on the French peasantry payment of an amount of interest equal to the annual interest on the entire British national debt. Small holding property, in this enslavement by capital to which its development inevitably pushes forward, has transformed the mass of the French nation into troglodytes. Sixteen million peasants (including women and children) dwell in hovels, a large number of which have but one opening, others only two and the most favoured only three. And windows are to a house what the five senses are to the head. The bourgeois order, which at the beginning of the century set the state to stand guard over the newly arisen small holding and manured it with laurels, has become a vampire that sucks out its blood and marrow and throws them into the alchemistic cauldron of capital. The *Code Napoléon**is now nothing but a *codex* of distraints, forced sales and compulsory auctions. To the four million (including children, etc.) officially recognised paupers, vagabonds, criminals and prostitutes in France, must be added five millions who hover on the margin of existence and either have their haunts in the countryside itself or, with their rags and their children, continually desert the countryside for the towns and the towns for the countryside. The interests of the peasants, therefore, are no longer, as under Napoleon, in accord with, but in opposition to the interests of the bourgeoisie, to capital. Hence the peasants find their natural ally and leader in the *urban proletariat*, whose task is the overthrow of the bourgeois order. But *strong and unlimited government*—and this is the second "*idée napoléonienne*," which the second Napoleon has to carry out—is called upon to defend by force this "material" order. This "material order" also serves as the catchword in all Bonaparte's proclamations against the rebellious peasants.

Besides the mortgage which capital imposes on it, the small holding is burdened by *taxes*. Taxes are the source of life for the bureaucracy, the army, the priests and the court, in short, for the whole apparatus of the executive power. Strong government and

---

* The code of civil laws of the French bourgeois state.—*Ed.*

8 K. Marx, the 18th Brumaire

THE EIGHTEENTH BRUMAIRE

heavy taxes are identical. By its very nature, small holding property forms a suitable basis for an all-powerful and innumerable bureaucracy. It creates a uniform level of relationships and persons over the whole surface of the land. Hence it also permits of uniform action from a supreme centre on all points of this uniform mass. It annihilates the aristocratic intermediate grades between the mass of the people and the state power. On all sides, therefore, it calls forth the direct interference of this state power and the intervention of its immediate organs. Finally, it produces an unemployed surplus population for which there is no place either on the land or in the towns, and which accordingly reaches out for state offices as a sort of respectable alms, and provokes the creation of state posts.

[Under Napoleon this numerous governmental personnel was not merely immediately productive, inasmuch as, through the means of compulsion of the state, it executed on behalf of the newly arisen peasantry, in the form of public works, etc., what the bourgeoisie could not yet accomplish by way of private industry. State taxes were a necessary means of compulsion to maintain exchange between town and country. Otherwise, the owner of a dwarf holding would in his rustic self-sufficiency have severed his connection with the townsman, as in Norway and a part of Switzerland.]

By the new markets which he opened at the point of the bayonet, and by the plundering of the Continent, Napoleon repaid the compulsory taxes with interest. These taxes were a spur to the industry of the peasant, whereas now they rob his industry of its last sources of aid and complete his powerlessness to resist pauperism. And an enormous bureaucracy, well-dressed and well-fed, is the *"idée napoléonienne"* which is most congenial of all to the second Bonaparte. How could it be otherwise, seeing that alongside the actual classes of society, he is forced to create an artificial caste, for which the maintenance of his regime becomes a bread-and-butter question? Accordingly, one of his first financial operations was the raising of officials' salaries to their old level again and the creation of new sinecures.

Another *"idée napoléonienne"* is the domination of the *priests* as a means of government. But if in its accord with society, in its dependence on natural forces and its subjection to the authority which protected it from above, the small holding that had newly come into being was naturally religious, the small holding that is ruined by debts, at odds with society and authority, and driven beyond its own limitations, naturally becomes irreligious. Heaven was quite a pleasing accessory to the narrow strip of land just won, more particularly as it makes the weather; it becomes an insult as soon as it is thrust forward as substitute for the small holding. The priest then appears as only the anointed bloodhound of the earthly police—another *"idée napoléonienne"*—[whose mission under the second Bonaparte is to keep watch over, not the enemies of the peasant regime in the towns, as under Napoleon, but the enemies of Bonaparte in the country]. On the next occasion, the expedition against Rome will take place in France itself, but in a sense opposite to that of M. de Montalembert.⁴²

Finally, the culminating point of the *'"idées napoléoniennes"* is the preponderance of the *army*. The army was the *point d'honneur* * of the peasants, it was they themselves transformed into heroes, defending their new possessions, against the outer world, glorifying their recently won nationality, plundering and revolutionising the world. The uniform was their own state dress; war was their poetry; the small holding, extended and rounded off in imagination, was their fatherland, and patriotism the ideal form of the property sense. But the enemies against whom the French peasant has now to defend his property are not the Cossacks; they are the *hussiers*** and the tax collectors. The small holding lies no longer in the so-called fatherland, but in the register of mortgages. The army itself is no longer the flower of the peasant youth; it is the swamp-flower of the peasant *lumpenproletariat*. It consists in large measure of *remplaçants*, of substitutes, just as the second Bonaparte is himself only a *remplaçant*, the substitute for Napoleon. It now performs its deeds of valour by hounding the peasants in masses like chamois, by discharging *gendarme* duties, and when the internal contradictions of his system chase the chief

---

* Point of honour.—*Ed.*
** Bailiffs.—*Ed.*

THE EIGHTEENTH BRUMAIRE

of the Society of December 10 over the French border, his army, after some acts of brigandage, will reap, not laurels, but thrashings.

One sees: *all* idées napoléoniennes *are the ideas of the undeveloped small holding in the freshness of its youth*: for the small holding that has outlived its day they are an absurdity. They are only the hallucinations of its death struggle, words that are reducèd to phrases, spirits reduced to ghosts. But the parody of imperialism was necessary to free the mass of the French nation from the weight of tradition and to work out in pure form the opposition between the state power and society. With the progressive undermining of this small holding property, the state structure erected upon it collapses. The state centralisation that modern society requires arises only on the ruins of the military-bureaucratic governmental machinery which was forged in opposition to feudalism.

[The demolition of the state machine will not endanger centralisation. Bureaucracy is only the low and brutal form of a centralisation that is still afflicted with its opposite, with feudalism. On coming to despair of the Napoleonic Restoration, the French peasant parts with his belief in his small holding, the entire state edifice erected on this small holding falls to the ground and the *proletarian revolution* obtains *that chorus without which its solo song in all peasant nations becomes a swan song.*]

French peasant relationships provide us with the answer to the riddle of the general elections of December 20 and 21, which bore the second Napoleon up Mount Sinai, not to receive laws, but to give them.

[To be sure, on those fateful days the French nation committed a deadly sin against democracy, which is on its knees and prays daily: Holy universal suffrage, intercede for us! Naturally, the believers in universal suffrage do not want to renounce a miraculous power that has accomplished such great things in regard to themselves, which has transformed Bonaparte II into a Napoleon, a Saul into a Paul and a Simon into a Peter. The spirit of the people speaks to them through the ballot-box as the god of the prophet Ezekiel spoke to the marrowless bones: *"Haec dicit*

OF LOUIS BONAPARTE

dominus deus ossibus suis: Ecce, ego intromittam in vos spiritum et vivetis." "Thus saith the Lord God unto these bones: Behold, I will cause breath to enter into you, and ye shall live."]

Manifestly, the bourgeoisie had now no choice but to elect Bonaparte. [Despotism or anarchy. Naturally, it voted for despotism.] When the puritans at the Council of Constance complained of the dissolute lives of the popes and wailed about the necessity of moral reform, Cardinal Pierre d'Ailly thundered to them: "Only the devil in person can now save the Catholic Church, and you ask for angels." In like manner, after the *coup d'état*, the French bourgeoisie cried: Only the chief of the Society of December 10 can now save bourgeois society! Only theft can now save property; only perjury, religion; only bastardy, the family; only disorder, order!

As the executive authority which has made itself an independent power, Bonaparte feels it to be his mission to safeguard "civil order." But the strength of this civil order lies in the middle class. He looks on himself, therefore, as the representative of the middle class and issues decrees in this sense. Nevertheless, he is somebody solely due to the fact that he has broken the political power of this middle class and daily breaks it anew. Consequently, he looks on himself as the adversary of the political and literary power of the middle class. But by protecting its material power, he generates its political power anew. The cause must accordingly be kept alive; but the effect, where it manifests itself, must be done away with. But this cannot pass off without slight confusions of cause and effect, since in their interaction both lose their distinguishing features. New decrees, that obliterate the border-line. At the same time, Bonaparte looks on himself as the representative of the peasants, and of the people in general, against the bourgeoisie, who wants to make the lower classes of the people happy within the frame of bourgeois society. New decrees, that cheat the "true socialists" of their statecraft in advance. But, above all, Bonaparte looks on himself as the chief of the Society of December 10, as the representative of the *lumpenproletariat* to which he himself, his *entourage*,* his government and his army belong, and for which

* Attendants.—*Ed.*

THE EIGHTEENTH BRUMAIRE

the prime consideration is to benefit itself and draw Californian lottery prizes from the state treasury. And he makes good his position as chief of the Society of December 10 with decrees, without decrees and despite decrees.

This contradictory task of the man explains the contradictions of his government, the confused groping hither and thither which seeks now to win, now to humiliate first one class and then another and arrays all of them uniformly against him, whose practical uncertainty forms a highly comical contrast to the imperious categorical style of the government decrees, a style which is copied obsequiously from the Uncle.

Industry and trade, hence the business affairs of the middle class, are to prosper in hot-house fashion under the strong government. Granting of innumerable railway concessions. But the Bonapartist *lumpenproletariat* is to enrich itself. Trickery with the railway concessions on the *Bourse* by those previously initiated. But no capital is forthcoming for the railways. Obligation of the Bank to make advances on railway shares. But, at the same time, the Bank is to be exploited for personal ends and therefore must be cajoled. Release of the Bank from the obligation to publish its report weekly. Leonine agreement* of the Bank with the government. The people are to be given employment. Inauguration of public works. But the public works increase the obligations of the people in respect of taxes. Therefore, reduction of the taxes by an onslaught on the *rentiers*,** by conversion of the five per cent bonds to four-and-a-half per cent. But, once more, the middle class must receive a sop. Therefore doubling of the wine tax for the people, who buy it *en détail*,*** and halving of the wine tax for the middle class, who drink it *en gros*.**** Dissolution of the actual workers' associations, but promises of miracles of association in the future. The peasants are to be helped. Mortgage banks, that expedite their getting into debts and accelerate the concentration of property. But these banks are to be used to make money out of the confiscated

---

* Meaning an agreement by which one gets the lion's share.—*Ed.*
** Persons drawing income from bonds and investments.—*Ed.*
*** Retail.—*Ed.*
**** Wholesale.—*Ed.*

OF LOUIS BONAPARTE

estates of the House of Orleans. No capitalist wants to agree to this condition, which is not in the decrees, and the mortgage bank remains a mere decree; etc. etc.

Bonaparte would like to appear as the patriarchal benefactor of all classes. But he cannot give to one class without taking from another. Just as at the time of the Fronde it was said of the Duke of Guise that he was the most *obligeant* * man in France because he had turned all his possessions into his partisans' obligations to him, so Bonaparte would fain be the most *obligeant* man in France and turn all the property, all the labour of France into a personal obligation to himself. He would like to steal the whole of France in order to be able to make a present of her to France or, rather, in order to be able to buy France anew with French money, for as the chief of the Society of December 10 he must needs buy what ought to belong to him. And all the state institutions, the Senate, the Council of State, the legislative body, the Legion of Honour, the soldier's medal, the wash-houses, the public works, the railways, the *état major*** of the National Guard to the exclusion of privates and the confiscated estates of the House of Orleans—all become parts of the institution of purchase. Every place in the army and in the government machine becomes a means for purchase. But the most important feature of this process, whereby France is taken in order to give to her, is the percentages that find their way to the head and the members of the Society of December 10 during the turnover. The witticism with which Countess L., the mistress of M. de Morny, characterised the confiscation of the Orleans estates: *"C'est le premier vol de l'aigle,"* *** is applicable to every flight of this *eagle*, which is more like a *raven*. He himself and his adherents call out to one another daily like that Italian Carthusian admonishing the miser who, with boastful display, counted up the goods on which he could yet live for years to come; *"Tu fai conto sopra i bene, bisogna prima far il conta sopra gli*

---

* Obliging.—*Ed.*
** Staff.—*Ed.*
*** "It is the first flight (theft) of the eagle." *Vol* means flight and theft. [*Note by F. Engels.*]

THE EIGHTEENTH BRUMAIRE

anni "* Lest they make a mistake in the years, they count the minutes. At the court, in the ministries, at the head of the administration and the army, a crowd of fellows pushes forward, of the best of whom it can be said that no one knows whence he comes, a noisy, disreputable, rapacious Bohème that dresses itself in gallooned coats with the same caricature of dignity as the high dignitaries of Soulouque. One can visualise clearly this upper stratum of the Society of December 10, if one reflects that *Veron-Crevel*** is its preacher of morals and *Granier de Cassagnac* its thinker. When Guizot, at the time of his ministry, utilised this Granier on a hole-and-corner newspaper against the dynastic opposition, he used to boast of him with the quip: "*C'est le roi des drôles,*" "he is the king of buffoons." One would do wrong to recall the Regency of Louis XV in connection with Louis Bonaparte's court and clique. For "often already, France has experienced a government of mistresses; but never before, a government of *hommes entretenus.*"***

Driven by the contradictory demands of his situation, and, at the same time, like a conjurer under the necessity of keeping the public gaze fixed on himself, as Napoleon's substitute, by constant surprises, hence of executing a *coup d'état en miniature***** every day, Bonaparte throws the entire bourgeois economy into confusion, lays hands on everything that seemed inviolable to the revolution of 1848, makes some tolerant of revolution, others desirous of revolution, and produces actual anarchy in the name of order, while at the same time he divests the whole state machine of its halo, profanes it and makes it at once loathsome and ridiculous. The cult of the Holy Coat at Treves [43] he duplicates at Paris in the cult of the Napoleonic imperial mantle. But if the imperial mantle finally falls on the shoulders of Louis Bonaparte, the iron statue of Napoleon will crash from the top of the Vendôme column.

* Thou countest thy goods, thou shouldst first count thy years.—*Ed.*

** In his *Cousine Bette*, Balzac delineates the thoroughly dissolute Parisian philistine in the character of Crevel, which he draws after the model of Dr. Veron, the proprietor of the *Constitutionnel*. [*Note by F. Engels.*]

*** Kept men. The words quoted are the words of Madame Girardin.— [*Note by F. Engels.*]

**** In miniature.—*Ed.*

EXPLANATORY NOTES

THE EIGHTEENTH BRUMAIRE OF LOUIS BONAPARTE

EXPLANATORY NOTES

1. The Vendôme column was erected in 1806-10, as a memorial to the victories of the "great army" of Napoleon I in 1805. It was cast from 1,200 cannon taken by Napoleon I in his battles with the Austrian and Russian armies. A statue of Napoleon I was erected at the top of the column. In the concluding sentence of *The Eighteenth Brumaire of Louis Bonaparte*, Marx predicts that Louis Bonaparte's coming to power would put an end to the cult of Napoleon I—the Napoleonic legend. It was not only in the sense of which Marx writes in his preface of 1869 that this prophecy came true. Fifteen months after Marx had written these lines, Louis Bonaparte was dethroned; and half a year after that the Vendôme column was destroyed, by decision of the Paris Commune (May 16, 1871), as a symbol of chauvinism and international enmity. After the defeat of the Commune, the column was restored.

2. The *Renaissance*—a cultural and historical period (from the fourteenth to the sixteenth centuries) marked by the appearance among progressive circles of West-European society of a special interest, unknown in the preceding period of the Middle Ages, in ancient Greek and Roman culture—literature, art, and philosophy. This interest was a result of the economic development of Western Europe, where the objective conditions in the fourteenth to sixteenth centuries were analogous to those which determined the flourishing of culture in the ancient world (money economy and the development of bourgeois relationships).

3. On the eighteenth of Brumaire (according to the calendar introduced in the period of the Great French Revolution), or November 9, 1799, Napoleon I carried out the *coup d'état* which concentrated supreme power in his hands; in 1804 he declared himself emperor. Thus, the republic—the most important political victory of the Great French Revolution—was destroyed. By "the second edition of the eighteenth Brumaire," Marx means the *coup d'état* accomplished by Louis Bonaparte, the nephew of Napoleon I, on December 2, 1851.

4. The Great English Revolution took place in about the middle of the seventeenth century. In this revolution, as Marx says, "the bourgeoisie was allied with the new nobility against the monarchy, the feudal nobility, and the ruling church." Oliver Cromwell was the greatest leader of these new classes that were struggling for power. In the course of the revolution, he established the dictatorship of these classes (the "Protectorate").

5. The day on which new presidential elections were to be held. Louis

THE EIGHTEENTH BRUMAIRE

Bonaparte would have had to retire on this day, as the constitution did not permit anyone to be elected to the presidency for a second time, except after an interval of four years.

6. The adherents of an ancient Christian sect, who believed in the second coming of Christ and in the establishment of the millennium, a thousand years of paradise on earth.

7. An old Roman story tells that once, when Rome was besieged, the sacred geese in the Roman fortress, the Capitol, wakened the garrison with their cackling; thanks to this, the garrison was able to beat off the attack of the enemies who had stolen up in the night.

8. This refers to the generals distinguished for their "great deeds" in Africa during the conquest of Algeria (Cavaignac, Changarnier, and others).

9. Here and elsewhere the square brackets in the text denote passages of the first edition omitted in subsequent editions.

10. The hero of Heine's poem, *Two Knights*. In this character, Heine ridicules the spendthrift Polish nobleman ("*Crapulinski*" comes from the French word *crapule*—gluttony, greediness). Here Marx means Louis Bonaparte.

11. On the morning of February 24, 1849, Louis Philippe, frightened at the revolutionary uprising, signed his abdication from the throne in favour of his grandson, the Count of Paris. In view of the latter's youth, it was proposed that his mother, the Duchess of Orleans, act as regent.

12. After the July Revolution in 1830, the revision of the constitution made almost no changes in the formerly existing suffrage. The electoral qualification was lowered only to 200 francs; and the age qualification was lowered from 40 to 30. Only 250,000 people, of the 34,000,000 people in France, had the right to vote.

13. *Prætorians* was the name given in ancient Rome to the personal body-guard of any general or emperor; this guard was in his pay, and was given various privileges. Mercenary, corrupt prætorians usually played a large part in the various palace revolutions. Here Marx is referring to the "*Society of the Tenth of December,*" the bodyguard of Louis Bonaparte.

14. On December 20, 1848, Louis Bonaparte appointed his first ministry, headed by **Odilon Barrot**.

15. The period of the Restoration—the period from the downfall of Napoleon I (1814) to the July Revolution of 1830, when the dynasty of the Bourbons, which had been overthrown by the Great French Revolution, was again in power. The supporters of this dynasty, which represented the interests of the big landowners, called themselves Legitimists (they considered the Bourbon monarchy the only legitimate government). The Orleanists were the supporters of the Orleans dynasty, which represented the interests of the bankers and the financial aristocrats, and which came into power after the July Revolution of 1830.

16. Caius Caligula—the third Roman emperor (37-41 A.D.). A crazy despot, put on the throne by the army. To humiliate the Senate—the shadowy

OF LOUIS BONAPARTE

remnant of the institutions of Republican Rome—he made his horse a senator.

17. The *Quæstors* (the bodyguard of the National Assembly). Generals Le Flo and Baze, brought in a bill by which the president of the National Assembly was to be entrusted with the preservation of the safety of the National Assembly, for which purpose he was to receive the right to call out military forces. This *Quæstors' Bill* was rejected on October 17, 1851, by a majority of 408 votes to 300.

18. The Fronde period in France—(1648-1653)—the period of the regency of Anne of Austria before Louis XIV came of age—a period characterised by the opposition movement of the so-called parliamentary Fronde and the Fronde princes. This movement, which was directed against the absolute power of the king, was extremely weak, petty and irresolute.

19. Schlemihl—the hero of "Peter Schlemihl," by Chamisso (1781-1838). He sold his shadow for wealth, and went seeking it all over the world.

20. At this time the revolutions in Italy, Hungary, and Germany had already suffered defeat. The last revolt—in Southern Germany (July and August, 1849)—was also defeated.

21. Ems was the seat of Count Chambord (afterwards Henry V)—the claimant to the French throne on the part of the Bourbon dynasty. His competitor of the Orleans dynasty (Louis Philippe), who had fled to England after the February revolution, lived at Claremont, near London. Thus, Ems and Claremont became the centres of the royalist intrigues.

22. After the events of June 13, forty deputies were brought to trial, one after the other. Some of the leaders of the Mountain fled (Ledru-Rollin, Felix Pyat and others); others were put into prison (as, for instance, the non-commissioned officers Rathier and Boichot).

23. In order to silence the republican opposition, a new ruling was adopted by the majority of the Assembly, limiting freedom of speech and subjecting the delegates to the direction of the president. Deputies could now be excluded from the Assembly and deprived of their salaries.

24. Near Austerlitz, a town in Moravia, Napoleon I won a great victory over the combined Russian and Austrian armies in 1805.

25. The temporary law against the press was issued on July 27. This law forbade the retail sale of newspapers without the permission of the administration: the latter could refuse this permission without giving any reasons. Any insult to the president of the republic was officially prosecuted. Any criticism of the laws was punished by fines, imprisonment, etc. The right of association—one of the most essential of the political victories of the February days—was abolished. By the new law on clubs, the government had the right to "close down clubs and existing unions which *might* be dangerous to public order." The state of siege was declared not only in Paris and its environs, but also in Lyons with five Departments, and in Strasbourg, Rheims, and other cities with sixteen Departments. Military courts functioned everywhere in place of the usual courts during the state of siege.

THE EIGHTEENTH BRUMAIRE

26. The *wine tax*, a burden falling on the poorest sections of the population, was revoked by the National Assembly with the intention of replacing it by an income tax. The first measure of the Fould ministry, appointed on November 1, 1849, was the re-establishment of the wine tax, in its former scandalous form, which made the tax fall mainly on the small consumers.

27. The *Education Law*, which was adopted by the National Assembly on March 16, 1850, put education as a whole in the hands of the Jesuit priests.

28. Marx in *The Holy Family* gives the following characterisation of the loan bank for the poor which was proposed by Eugene Sue in his *Mysteries of Paris*.

"The idea of the critical Poor Bank, if otherwise taken as reasonable, reduces itself to the following. From the pay of the worker during the period when he is employed there is to be withdrawn as much as he needs to live on in the period of unemployment. Whether I advance him a definite sum in the unemployed period and he gives me this sum back when employed, or whether he gives up a definite sum when employed and I return it to him in the period of unemployment, is one and the same. He always gives me in his employed period what he receives from me in his unemployed period."

29. Burgrave—a sarcastic nickname, which referred to the impotent love of power and feudal ambitions of the monarchists; borrowed from a play by Victor Hugo.

30. Louis Bonaparte's first unsuccessful attempt at a *coup d'état* occurred in 1836, in Strasbourg. The invasion of Boulogne—his second unsuccessful attempt to proclaim himself emperor—was in 1840.

31. *Alexander of Macedonia* (356-323 B.C.) was famous for his conquering expeditions into Asia.

According to the Greek myth *Bacchus* (or Dionysus), the ancient Greek god of the vine, went all over Asia with a drunken retinue.—*Ed*.

32. Marx is referring to the parliaments of pre-revolutionary France, which were supreme courts. They had the right to register new royal decrees; in case of disagreement, they could only present a remonstrance to the king, requesting that the decree be revoked.

33. This refers to the struggle during the restoration period between Louis XVIII, who resided in the Palace of the Tuileries, and the representatives of the even more reactionary policy of the Comte d'Artois (afterwards King Charles X), who lived in the Pavillon Marsan, in the Palace of the Tuileries.

34. Marx's ironic term for the corrupt court ladies and gentlemen. Vestals was the name given in the ancient world to the priestesses of the goddess Vesta, who took the vow of chastity. The Paladins were the wandering knights of the Middle Ages who were shining examples of knightly valour.

35. Marx calls Thorigny's ministry a fictitious one, inasmuch as it was made up of the so called "Elysian brotherhood"—*i.e.*, Bonaparte's personal adherents.

36. Masaniello (1623-1647)—a fisherman, the leader of an uprising against the Spanish dominion in Naples, in 1647.

OF LOUIS BONAPARTE

37. The first world-wide Industrial Exhibition took place in London, May 1 to October 11, 1851.

38. The name given to an English parliament of the period of the Great English Revolution, which met for 13 years (1640-1653). Cromwell established his dictatorship in 1653, and dissolved this parliament.

39. In his classic work, *The State and Revolution,* Lenin cites this section of *The Eighteenth Brumaire* and writes: "In this remarkable passage Marxism makes a tremendous step forward in comparison with the position of *The Communist Manifesto.* There the question of the state still is treated extremely in the abstract, in the most general terms and expressions. Here the question is treated in a concrete manner, and the conclusion is most precise, definite, practical and palpable: all revolutions which have taken place up to the present have helped to perfect the state machinery, whereas it must be smashed, broken to pieces.

"This conclusion is the chief and fundamental thesis in the Marxist theory of the state. Yet it is this fundamental thesis which has been not only completely *forgotten* by the dominant official Social-Democratic parties, but directly *distorted* (as we shall see later) by the foremost theoretician of the Second International, K. Kautsky.

"In *The Communist Manifesto* are summed up the general lessons of history, which force us to see in the state the organ of class domination, and lead us to the inevitable conclusion that the proletariat cannot overthrow the bourgeoisie without first conquering political power, without obtaining political rule, without transforming the state into the proletariat organised as the ruling class; and that this proletarian state will begin to wither away immediately after its victory, because in a society without class antagonisms, the state is unnecessary and impossible. The question as to how, from the point of view of historical development, this replacement of the capitalist state by the proletarian state shall take place, is not raised here.

"It is precisely this question that Marx raises and solves in 1852. True to his philosophy of dialectical materialism, Marx takes as his basis the historical experience of the great revolutionary years 1848-51. Here, as everywhere, his teaching is the *summing up of experience,* illuminated by a profound philosophical world conception and a rich knowledge of history." (*Collected Works,* Vol. XXI, Book II, pp. 171-172.)

40. In Cevennes (Southern France, Languedoc), at the beginning of the eighteenth century, there was an uprising of protestant peasants under the slogans, "Down with taxes! Freedom of faith!"

The Vendée peasantry was the most backward at the time of the Great French Revolution; it supported the monarchist counter-revolution.

41. The *Convention*—the revolutionary representative assembly of the Great French Revolution. It was created in September 1792, after the overthrow of the monarchy and the establishment of the republic. Its majority was controlled by the Jacobins—the representatives of the revolutionary petty bour-

THE EIGHTEENTH BRUMAIRE

geoisie. The Convention carried through dictatorially all the revolutionary measures of the Great Revolution.

42. Montalembert, the head of the militant Catholic party, spoke, during the discussions on universal suffrage, on the necessity of undertaking a Roman expedition "within" France—meaning support of the Roman Pope and the Catholic clergy. Marx, on the other hand, is speaking of an expedition against Rome in the sense of a struggle *against* the clergy.

43. One of the "sacred" relics ("the vestment of the Lord"), exhibited in the Treves cathedral in 1844, for public worship.